A Decade of Still Life

Photo by Edwin Stein

A Decade of Still Life | Aaron Bohrod

The University of Wisconsin Press
Madison, Milwaukee, and London, 1966

Published by
The University of Wisconsin Press
Madison, Milwaukee, and London
U.S.A.: Box 1379, Madison, Wisconsin 53701
U.K.: 26-28 Hallam Street, London, W. 1

Composition by Graphco, Inc., Neenah, Wisconsin
Offset printing by the Meriden Gravure Co., Meriden, Connecticut
Gravure by Joh. Enschedé en Zonen, Haarlem, Holland
Binding by the George Banta Co., Inc., Menasha, Wisconsin

Library of Congress Catalog Card Number 66-10492

This book is for Ruth, my wife.
Since it will probably be
my only venture into full-scale book publication,
I also dedicate it
to our children Mark, Georgi Faye,
and Neil Franklin.

Preface

In as close a chronology as the exigencies of book-making will allow, the bulk of this book reflects my first decade of interest in still-life painting. It contains almost all of the principal efforts of the years 1954 through 1964. Omitted were only a very small number of works which were not contemporaneously photographed and where the present ownership is not known to me. Also omitted were a few works of small format where the photographs were of poor quality or were not available.

Unless otherwise described as to materials or technique, the originals of the reproductions in this book are in oil on gesso panels. All dimensions are given in inches, with the vertical dimension preceding the horizontal dimension.

In a number of cases where it was possible to make them so, the reproductions are in the exact size of the original works.

I want to thank the collectors who took the trouble to ship their paintings to Madison to be photographed in color. To Mr. George Gambsky of the University of Wisconsin Photographic Laboratory goes my gratitude for his tireless efforts in recording in faithful color the paintings for which plates were engraved in the Netherlands by Enschedé en Zonen. Mr. Gambsky should be credited with all the color photography except for a single plate executed by the Detroit Art Institute of a painting in its own collection.

I am very grateful, too, for the work done by the staff of the University of Wisconsin Photographic Laboratory over a long period of time on paintings of the still-life variety and on much of the earlier work contained in the text section. In this connection I wish especially to thank Mr. Clarence Kailin, who printed most of the black-and-white photographs.

Finally I wish to express sincere thanks to my editor, Miss Joan M. Krager, and to the designer of the book, Mr. William Nicoll, to President Fred Harrington of the University of Wisconsin, and to Mr. Thompson Webb, Jr., director of the University of Wisconsin Press, all of whom have made this book possible.

List of Titles

Prologue

I was born on the near west side of Chicago on November 21, 1907. As a child of three or four, I found the first outlet for my eternally gnawing bug of art expression — filling countless 2¢ plain yellow paper pads with all kinds of pencil scratchings. My mother used to tell me that all she needed to assure my contribution to domestic tranquility was to provide me with such a tablet. Faithfully, both sides of each sheet were filled with small-scale aesthetic evidence of, perhaps, better things to come. I wish some of these documents of presumed talent had been preserved. I suppose that some of my childish scrawls were imitative of a calligraphic, continuous line bird which was my Bessarabian-born father's sole achievement in the plastic arts and

1

which my brother Milton and my sisters Anne and Lillian also attempted to reproduce. I recall that on transparent chewing-gum wrappers I first traced the comic-strip characters of the day, and later with growing confidence copied them. The coloring book or two which came my way was filled in with shadings of gray pencil tones instead of the usual colored wax crayons, which had not yet been discovered by my family.

During the war years of 1914 to 1918 I was the most ardent producer of posters advertising war savings stamps in my school (La Fayette on the northwest side). While my numerous pictorial exhortations were blatant and generously colored, my own parentally controlled monetary contributions in this area were on a painfully miserly scale. The socialistic leanings of my parents, who felt that any enemy of czarist Russia should be no particular enemy of ours, made it difficult for them to be certain that we were on the right side in the conflict; and they were poor, if not miserably poor.

Since this writing purports only to set the stage for presentation of my current work, I do not intend to detail the joys and the aches and the growing pains of childhood or of my later life. Nor is this the place to describe the fortunes or all the peregrinations of the Bohrod family.

My father was a cigar maker who suffered one labor strike too many. In about 1919 he started out on his own in the business world. He bought a small grocery store on St. Louis Avenue and 13th Place. I led an alternately miserable and reasonably content existence in the store. Delivering orders interfered with a more or less normal boy's absorption with baseball, but my brother and I found one compensation in presenting an imaginative weekly display of our grocery wares in a corner of the St. Louis Avenue show window. It was rewarding to watch the casual passerby stopped by the view of an unusual juxtaposition of offerings, of shapes echoed by related shapes, of materials stacked in strange order. These window displays were the first still-life arrangements I attempted.

When my brother emerged from Crane Tech to become a full-fledged pre-medical student, I followed him into that school. Since I did not think he had noticed my artistic propensities, he once amazed and gratified me by the gift of an almost professional watercolor box. After a year or two I decided I cared for not much of anything in the school curriculum but drawing. School art offerings were slim, but I delighted in both mechanical and freehand drawing. A short term in children's Saturday classes at the Chicago Art Institute, where I first discovered the paintings in the upstairs collections, and an abortive correspondence art-school course perhaps furthered my art education.

This education began seriously in 1926, after I had spent an aimless term in the city college then attached to Crane, and after a series of jobs allowed me to scrape together the funds necessary to enter art school. At this period my parents neither encouraged me nor placed obstacles in the way of my plans. Later my father's indifference was to turn to vehement partisanship whenever the public press noted my Chicago-exhibited paintings with any sentiment other than outright praise.

I survived four years of art-school training. This comprised two chopped-up years at the school of the Chicago Art Institute, where I acquired everything in aesthetic education but real painting experience, and two even more fragmented years at the Art Students League in New York. New York gave me the opportunity to work with some outstanding teachers: Boardman Robinson, John Sloan, Kenneth Hayes Miller, Charles Locke, and Richard Lahey. While they were all helpful, it was John Sloan who fired me most with the desire to find a way through the growth of art movements which was jungle-like even then. Sloan was an inspiring teacher. He had the ability to reveal to his students the beauties of the old masters and at the same time to cause them to open their eyes to the visual world as the basic raw material for incipient art expression.

Sloan's early paintings of New York streets, back yards, restaurants, and waterfronts pointedly dramatized for me the artist's ability to take subjects from the commonplace and transform them through his gifted perception into beautiful and meaningful works of art.

Almost the first activity I engaged in on returning to Chicago in 1930 was entering the first of the Depression-inspired outdoor exhibitions held in Grant Park on the grass outside the Art Institute. I had brought from New York many color sketches of cityscapes, harbors, and subway low life. My wife and I scattered these on the Institute's august lawn which, probably in contempt, curled the

Chicago Street, 1930
pencil drawing, 10½ x 12½

Greenwich Village Gas Station, 1930
opaque tempera, 16¾ x 12

pictures into tight, moist scrolls. Unfurled once more, these studies launched my professional life.

The color sketches and small watercolors were things that I had turned out in prodigious quantity in my New York rooming house. Sometimes I produced seven or eight of them in one evening. For a time I overwhelmed Sloan with the task of criticism by volume. After a bad start with him — he complained often of the slick wrist which played over my classroom studies — he told me he had begun to see merit in some of my work. He said he saw promise of interesting picture ideas, of fresh vision.

At the open-air show I sold thirty or forty of these sketches for about two dollars each. My chief presentation, a reasonably well-framed watercolor, brought five dollars. The excitement of being among real artists and the beginnings of lifelong friendships with such other exhibitors as Francis Chapin, Edgar Britton, Constantine Pougialis, William Schwartz, and Ivan and Malvin Albright counted as real reward for me.

Though the times were lean, there seemed promise in life for the artist in Chicago. I was determined to do in my own way with my own city what Sloan had done with New York. For many years, then, Chicago was the focus of my painting world. I haunted its shabby streets and alleys, jotting down perfunctory idea notes or, with a more elaborate catalogue of visual elements, getting down on my sketchbook pages the subjects that would serve as reference for the creation of complete works in gouache and in oil.

In the young painter ideas and energy abound. While my wife earned our bread by teaching in the city's schools, it was not unusual for me to dash off a few watercolors or a gouache in the morning and top off the day's endeavor with a completely finished oil in the remaining afternoon and evening. This was regular practice for the earliest months of my professional painting life. Days of sketching on city streets alternated with intense and frenzied activity at my easel.

In one of the early years, 1933, I think I must have produced several hundred full-scale works. Most of my

Clifton Park "El" Platform, 1930
gouache, about 14 x 22

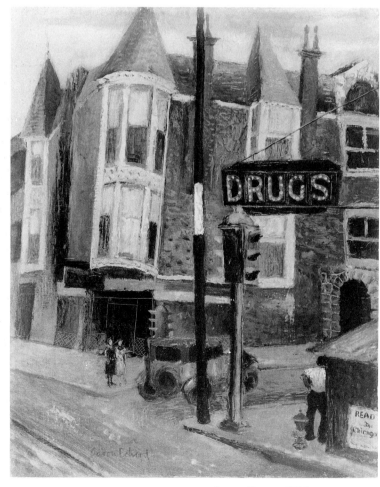

Street Corner, 1930
oil, 20 x 16

Football, 1932
oil, 18 x 24

subjects were, of course, the sometimes teeming and sometimes bleak streets of Chicago. But also into my work I put views of the city beaches and the burlesque theatre, where I did some post-graduate life study, park landscapes, figures, interiors, and even experiments in abstract painting. Later I was to decry the emptiness of the abstract form. But I could not publicly proclaim this fault without having experimented in the idiom to see what it might have held in promise for my own development.

In the way of figure painting my work of that time had a leaning toward caricature and toward the expressionism which was widely manifest, especially in the works of European artists who were becoming known in this country. I executed every conceivable kind of painting but the still life which has been my engrossing interest for the last ten years. Especially in the watercolor variety of my early work I was deeply enamored of the "effects" available to the painter. For instance, a pen heavily charged with colored ink, drawn and scraped through the wet opaque ground of tempera, resulted in a completely fascinating blur of color bleeding outward from the inked furrow. Inordinately excited interest in technique was undeservedly stressed, perhaps, to the detriment of other necessary elements in a painting's make-up. However, I was never so far from what the visual setting meant to me that I allowed the varied technical investigation to smother the subject which, in all my works, was essentially man and his environment.

My painting production did not diminish the ardent faithfulness with which I pursued a love for drawing fostered under the tutelage of John Sloan. Sloan had been a nut on drawing. To him painting was only drawing with oil color. "Draw," he said, "draw everything you *see* or *imagine* or *dream of,* and draw in every conceivable way and with every conceivable tool." And so we students drew. At night, in our rooms, we turned out the lights and drew strange things without being able to see our paper. We drew from memory. We drew with the left hand.

Burlesque, 1933
gouache, 14 x 20

Sister Act, 1933
tempera and ink, 15 x 20

North Avenue Beach, 1933
gouache, 15 x 20½

We drew with both hands at once. We pretended we were Renoir and drew like him. Like Picasso. Like Matisse. Always this was supposed to be done consciously as exercise, with an effort to fathom the artist's thought processes, never with the idea of acquiring style cheaply.

Residing in a kind of colony in a studio building on North Avenue in Chicago where each artist-family occupied a single studio space that was at once bedroom, living room, kitchen, and workshop, a group of the artist-residents gathered in one of the studios several nights each week to pursue the delineation of the human figure. I set down hundreds of drawings in my sketchbooks. The drive for this kind of plastic expression has never abated for me. Occasionally such a sketch would serve as the basis for a work in a heavier, more complex medium, but most of the time I was content merely to be drawing for the sake of drawing.

Wherever I went, I was never without some kind of sketchbook. Apart from the posed figure and the passing scene gleaned from the streets, countless pictorial ideas, intriguing details, informal figure arrangements, useful and useless doodles found repository in these books. Drawing, I have always thought, is the best way for the artist to build his visual vocabulary. Until the advent of the completely abstract painting which decreed the abolition of drawing as an element of art, powerful draughtsmanship was the attribute which set the true artist apart from the dilettante.

The constant and quick flow of picture ideas was valuable in that it got me over that troublesome hump: what *is* there to paint? I have never been at a loss for some kind of subject matter. We live in a visually exciting world. It is strange that many artists today cannot discuss this world in paint. They feel that to be truly creative they must turn their backs to the world and produce only a nothingness which does not relate to visual life.

The artist — if he will amount to anything — constantly revolts against the going thing in art. Often he even reacts against his own impulses when they have held sway for a long enough while. After several years of work

Abstraction, 1933
oil, 10 x 12

Nude, 1932
oil on canvas panel, 16 x 20

The Chat, 1933
gouache and colored ink, 9¼ x 12¼

The Bride, 1932
gouache, 14 x 10

Head, 1932
tempera and ink, 9 x 5½

in which technical interests had loomed unduly large, I felt that corrective measures must be taken with my painting if it were not to dissolve in pure sensation. I began, then, a series of tightly controlled studies that consciously opposed the informally organized, sometimes primitive-looking statements that preceded them. Stick by stick and brick by brick I built my work on a rigid scaffold of conscious design which supported in regulated manner the new approach I took.

One cannot have at once spontaneity and precise order. Conscious order was what I was after and in its favor I set aside the alluring splash and flow of runny pigment. One of the works in the hard-boiled vein was "Landscape near Chicago," a Skokie Valley setting which was shown at the Whitney Museum of American Art in New York. A Chicago newspaper with mild indignation reproduced the painting under the heading "New York's view of Chicago." The few bristling protests the notice evoked neither deterred nor specifically encouraged additional investigation of the city's auto graveyards and other unprepossessing places. These were simply some of the unlovely subjects that interested me. I have always felt that intrinsic beauty in a subject is a handicap when the artist selects a motif for his work. What can an artist really say about a beautiful sunset that would improve on nature; about a brand new, shining automobile; about a newly completed chunk of modern architecture? It is probably incorrect to say that no artist under any set of circumstances can use these motifs well, but it *is* fair to say that, unlike those things affectionately or mercilessly touched by time, the brisk, the new, and the beautiful are not very *likely* subjects for the artist.

Apart from its usefulness in drawings for their own sake and in the quick setting down of preliminary picture ideas, spontaneity is a vastly overrated attribute in the construction of a full-scale painting. The paintings executed

North Side, Chicago, 1933
gouache and colored ink, 14 x 20

Sketch Group, 1934
oil, 19 x 24

Drawing, 1933
colored ink washes, 11 x 8¼

Drawing, 1933
pen and ink, about 10 inches high

in 1934 and for a year or two afterward demanded from me a concentrated and thoughtful arrangement of visual materials. The precise decision of response required for them provided the foundation on which my present work in still life rests and made possible, also, several intervening ways of setting down the look and feel of life.

In the early years, diverse periods of painting come thick and fast for the artist. For one thing, he is never certain for long that he is on the right road, that what he is doing is what he wants to be doing for all time. The struggle for individual style is the great bugaboo of the art student and of the young professional. Only when he ceases the self-conscious search for style and loses himself in subject matter that grips him does his painting style emerge. But the artist should never be unaware that his painting can fall into an unwelcome run of stale mannerism.

After carrying on my stringent course of careful construction for quite a period, I felt that aridity threatened to overtake this severely managed painting, that an infusion of the former gay recklessness might cause the work to pulsate once more. A reversion to the earlier work — more colorful and less severely designed, but based on a new sense of composition developed through the recent period of disciplined endeavor — should, I thought, have tonic effect. I embarked on an altered course where I tried to combine the merits of the two preceding styles. The results appeared satisfying to the extent that I could relegate the idea of style to the subconscious mind. I felt that I could devote myself entirely to the more important tasks of devouring my subjects, analyzing and interpreting them, and distilling the results into meaningful art expression.

At the Rehn Gallery in New York I had had two one-man shows notable for their evocation of faint printed praise and no sales. The exhibitions had been useful, however, in making my work known to the strong group of painters connected with that gallery. Alexander Brook,

Clark Street, Chicago, 1934
oil, 24 x 32

Landscape near Chicago, 1934
oil, 24 x 32

Tourist Cabin, 1936
oil, 22 x 26

Eugene Speicher, Reginald Marsh, and Edward Hopper had looked on my work, I was informed, not entirely with disdain. I was emboldened to prevail on them for recommendations to the Guggenheim Foundation. A fellowship grant would give me the assurance of continuing my work without the troublesome economic strain that most artists suffer from at some stage in their careers. Some financial support had come my way through participation in W.P.A. art projects and through the winning of mural competitions for post offices. These were helpful, but the atmosphere of political push and pull surrounding these projects was not eminently satisfactory. Marsh modestly told me that his recommendation to the Guggenheim would be a kiss of death, but I felt I had everything to gain by it.

The fellowship came with all the fanfare that attended the activity of the foundation's early years of existence. It allowed me to expand my horizons outward from Chicago. While I had submitted a plan for study which called for European travel, I really had not cared much about going abroad. What I wanted to do was paint, and what I wanted to paint was my own country. This attitude was undoubtedly influenced by the tremendous interest in what was called the "American Scene." The triumvirate of so-called regional painters — Tom Benton, Grant Wood, and John Steuart Curry — had become the best known, the most admired, and the most discussed painters this country had ever known. They constituted the first real art movement that captured the attention of the American public. Though some worldly critics claimed there was nothing really new in all this, the public *was* getting its first look at American rural life portrayed with skill, sympathy, and an insight of restrained emotion.

For a good long while these three swept most of the nation's artists along with them. Any painter's mere decision to depict a red barn almost automatically qualified him for serious attention. Conversely, after the inevitable

Peoria Street, ca. 1939
gouache, about 15 x 20

New Orleans Sidewalk, 1937
oil, about 20 x 27

Wyoming Landscape, 1936
reed and ink drawing, 10½ x 14¾

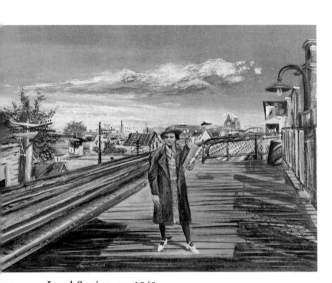

Local Station, ca. 1940
gouache, about 14 x 20

reaction set in, any artist's desire to portray a red barn disqualified him from consideration as a creative worker and relegated him to the role of flag-waver and jingo.

Essentially the example of the regionalists was sound. After all, Cézanne had not chosen to paint Pittsburgh, nor had Canaletto painted the Congo. These and many other artists had depended on the life around them for visual sustenance.

The unrest on the Continent engendered by the Spanish Civil War in 1936 allowed me to beg off Europe and spend the first year of my grant in sketch travel to the western reaches of the country. From Wyoming I brought back sketches resulting in paintings that won awards in the Carnegie International Exhibition in 1939 and in the American show at the Chicago Art Institute in 1937. The latter painting, "Wyoming Landscape," of a ramshackle filling station backed by a low range of mountains was immediately rated by the sponsor of this top award, Mrs. Frank Logan, as "not worth a nickel."

Notoriety of this kind helps a painter's career. If he does not allow himself to brood over the negative qualities or to become inordinately elated over the beneficial aspects, he finds his work is looked at with more attention. While he cannot hope to attain universal acclaim, he finds his sympathetic observers become more sympathetic and understanding, even if his detractors become more vehement in their reactions.

A renewal of the Guggenheim allowed investigation of the landscape of the eastern sections of the country. Visits to art colonies expanded acquaintance among practicing artists and knowledge of the workings of the art world. When the Associated American Artists made vigorous entry onto the New York art scene and when Grant Wood, whom I had come to know, suggested to its director that I might be suitable material for it, I began to experience the first genuine acceptance that had come my way.

Beyond the value of moderate public acceptance the gallery was able to elicit, membership provided me with the opportunity to meet and on occasion to work with some of the artists I had long admired. Adolf Dehn, Georges

Waiting for the 3:30, ca. 1940
oil on gesso panel, about 27 x 36

Little Circus, ca. 1946
oil on gesso panel, 24 x 32

Pennsylvania Highway, ca. 1940
oil on gesso panel, 18 x 24

Dunes Landscape, 1938
oil on gesso panel, 24 x 32

Children in Costume, 1947
oil on gesso panel, about 28 x 33

Schreiber, Raphael Soyer, Paul Sample, George Grosz, Doris Lee, Arnold Blanch, Tom Benton, John Steuart Curry, Grant Wood, Joe Jones, Joseph Hirsch, Lawrence Beall Smith, Fred Taubes, Marion Greenwood, together with almost too many other respectable artists, were all members of the gallery. They made a concentrated group of talented people as strong as any America has known. Overweighted, finally, on the side of putting the membership's talents to use too often in the commercial world through some good and some unworthy projects, and with a change in the kind of art it became fashionable to profess liking for, the gallery could not make up its mind which way it wanted to go. A last-gasp flirtation with Johnny-come-lately practitioners of the abstract (the "giants" of the movement who had registered their trademarks had all found homes in other galleries) did not work out. As a place for the presentation of painting and sculpture, the gallery teetered and fell apart in 1956.

With my entry into the Associated American Artists in 1939 while in the midst of a kind of work that maintained a reasonable control but was warmed by a certain romantic glow, I found that my work was gaining a little attention from collectors — or at least from sensitive people who enjoyed having paintings in their homes. Gratifying as this attention was, there was at the same time a lurking danger in the production of the kind of painting that proves appealing primarily on the grounds of subject matter or of mood. One such area was the winter landscape where a darkling sky might set off the snowy whites of foreground to produce a pigmented concoction of mouth-watering quality. Such a painting, if cleanly and proficiently executed, was almost inevitably a likeable one.

Another subject which proved dangerously successful was, in my case, the artificially illuminated night scene. For a time the neon-lighted street was a compelling interest.

19

City Park, Winter, 1947
oil on gesso panel, about 14 x 19

Neon Nocturne, ca. 1940
oil on gesso panel, about 18 x 14

Illinois Farm, ca. 1946
gouache, about 16 x 23½

La Salle at Night, ca. 1939
oil on gesso panel, 16 x 20

Sketch for La Salle at Night, ca. 1939
pencil, 7½ x 10¼

These neon nocturnes, with streets and people bathed in pink and green glow and with the strange light sometimes reflected on wet pavement, exacted my own prolonged attention and met with a public response which for the first time could be described as eager. After *Life* magazine had published (in 1941) a color story on my nighttime oils, wherein they pigeonholed me in a compartment where I had little competition and then characterized me as "America's No. 1 painter of neon lights," the demand for these works as relayed by the New York gallery became so great that I feared long continuance would lead to the sterile business of order-filling. I called a halt to the inclination before I felt that I had said the last word on the subject.

Often my work has fallen into series of paintings where the execution of one promising result opens possibilities of interesting variation. In this way over a number of years I created a series of what I called "Nudes and Masterpieces." I believe the first on this theme was suitably an Eve: a female nude flanked by a delicate table, on which rested an apple, stood against a freely brushed representation of the Massaccio expulsion from Eden. This was followed by some dozen or more similar efforts, all in small format. The

Reflections on a Shop Window, ca. 1941
oil on gesso panel, 18 x 24

Antiques, ca. 1947
oil on gesso panel, 18 x 24

Bather, ca. 1939
oil on gesso panel, 16 x 12

Girl with Bird, ca. 1946
oil on gesso panel, 16 x 12

scattered collection contained an Amazon with the Courbet painting of the same applied name, several Venus versions with inspiration from Botticelli and Velasquez, a bather with Renoir, and so on. I have heard of a collector in Kansas City who is attempting to bring all these little works together under one roof, his own. I wish him well, though the spread of the works makes the task a formidable one.

Another vein of recurrent interest which I struck was the antique-shop window. With landscape or opposing street often reflected from the shimmering surface of the glass window pane, I depicted jumbled bric-a-brac in a kind of come-and-go of fascinating color, now realizing, now vaguely suggesting the elusive beauty of these sometimes junky objects. In a way these paintings stand as forerunner to my present work, though I did not then think to let the objects serve in a symbolic sense.

Before the Associated folded as a picture gallery, its director, Reeves Lewenthal, arranged a number of highly creditable projects with magazines, department stores, and the U.S. Corps of Engineers. Just when World War II began, Lewenthal and George Biddle had thought to interest the government in sending civilian artists abroad to use the talents of men in the armed forces to record the war in terms of painting. A project Life magazine had broached to me and which I was eager to begin, that of going to Russia as an artist–war correspondent, seemed just too complex for them to work out. Arrangements were so prolonged and unpromising that I accepted an offer to go to the Pacific in a War Art Unit organized by the U.S. Engineers.

After the war, the best of the projects arranged by Lewenthal, together with Estelle Mandel and Robert Parsons, involved selecting a city or state locale and turning loose on it a dozen or so artists to record aesthetically those aspects of the setting that most interested them. Usually the project was sponsored by a large department store that received value in free advertising as well as possession of some fairly good pieces of painting. I think I worked on most of these

The Lake, Michigan, ca. 1947
oil on gesso panel, 24 x 32

Alleyway, Pittsburgh, ca. 1946
oil on gesso panel, 20 x 16

projects doing, in turn, paintings of Fifth Avenue for a New York City collection, Kansas City for a Missouri project, Pittsburgh for a Pennsylvania project, and the vacation spots of the state in a roving assignment for a Michigan project. Opportunities for travel made it possible to utilize leftover material for additional works outside the scope of the projects.

In 1942, my wife, my eight-year-old son Mark, and I were living in Carbondale, where I occupied the post of artist-in-residence at what was then Southern Illinois Normal University. The first and most outstanding of such residencies was that established by the College of Agriculture at the University of Wisconsin for John Curry in 1936. The success of the experiment interested other colleges and universities. They were beginning to make such appointments and were engaged in little flurries of talent search within the framework of grants from the Carnegie Foundation. I was not well enough known to have been noticed by any major school, but the then small S.I.N.U. through its enterprising art department director, Burnett Shryock, and a very progressive president, Roscoe Pulliam, had made a hit with the Carnegie people by proposing to create a residency for me. Primarily, I think, the idea received approval because the school volunteered to pay half the costs involved.

The situation at Carbondale was a happy one. I got to know many townspeople and students interested in art. Though a light teaching load had been added to my duties, in the six months I spent there I was able to accomplish quite a few paintings of a very interesting locale. Weekly open-house sessions at my studio, where I had to learn to explain and defend myself, were invaluable in formulating self-knowledge and establishing a maturity of attitude regarding my own work. It was my intention to get back to

Dark Sunday, ca. 1942
gouache, about 14 x 18

Solitaire, 1943
pen and ink and wash, 9¼ x 11

Gibbs Grocery, Carbondale, ca. 1942
oil on gesso panel, 16 x 20

Carbondale after the war to round out the residency and to engage in a second-year renewal which had already been arranged. However strong the intention, plans cannot always be fulfilled and I did not find it possible to resume the position.

The war brought many opportunities to me as an artist. At the age of thirty-five when my war-art period began, it would not have been expected that I'd be drafted for active military service. Most likely, instead of a gun I would have been handed a broom to sweep up some domestic army barracks. I preferred a paint brush to a scrub brush. That I was allowed to paint at all during those hectic times proved to be the greatest gift of all. The opportunity to share in part, at least, the life of the fighting soldier and to gain close insight into the miseries and the occasional glories of combat made possible the basic understanding essential to pictorial interpretation.

With the War Art Unit of soldiers and civilians organized by the U.S. Engineers I spent five or six exciting weeks in San Francisco while awaiting Pacific transportation. The briefings, medical preparation, gathering of supplies — combined with the task of partially inuring myself to what has always been hateful to me, paperwork and red tape — were interspersed with an orgy of social activity, a kind of last fling before the deluge of war reality. Our three-man unit was led by Howard Cook, a civilian like myself, and also included Sgt. Charles Shannon. When we branched off from the larger body of collected artists to go to the South Pacific, we were accompanied by David Fredenthal, who was appointed to Australia. Fredenthal, who accomplished some of the most stirring paintings of the war, attached himself to us for the trip and for several weeks afterward.

A three-week trip by Dutch steamship was enlivened by only one small submarine scare. Finding diversion in several thousand models engaged in interesting human activity, we also held lively aesthetic debates to keep ourselves entertained. Finally, we set up our first studio camp outside Noumea in New Caledonia, where we fought losing battles with the Army to establish for Charley Shannon's sake the principle of equal rights for *all* war artists even if they *were* enlisted men. We spent some

C-Rations, 1943
gouache, about 17 x 14

Rendova Rendezvous, 1943
oil on panel, 16 x 20

Moving Up, Rendova, 1943
gouache, about 14 x 17

weeks digesting rumors of impending violent activity
while we eased into the theme of war art through the development of paintings based on the long steamer trip.

The island of New Caledonia, and especially the little
metropolis of Noumea, was a colorful place. However,
the artist–war correspondent, like his writer counterpart,
quickly learns to gauge the value of his surroundings by
the degree of the heat of war, and New Caledonia was not
a violently threatened area. After a decent interval we
moved on to some of the Solomon Islands, then to a stay
in Guadalcanal, which had been almost entirely cleared of
Japanese. Here we awaited participation in the movement
into new, enemy-occupied territory. This, for me, proved
to be the invasion of Rendova Island across from the
Japanese airfield in Munda. The experience resulted in
camera records and sketches which provided some dramatic evidence of the dank, wet, miserable struggle to remain alive while inflicting as much damage as possible on
the enemy. On returning to New Caledonia and while I
was excitedly working up my material into form for de-
livery to Washington, we received disturbing news from
home. The very modest financial allotment for the support
of the War Arts Unit had not escaped the scrutiny of an
obscure congressman, who made a twenty-four hour name
for himself by having it struck out of the vast appropria-
tions that admittedly incorporated millions in waste. Our
fears that we'd be stranded in the Pacific, or at least be
subject to immediate recall, were ended when *Life* magazine and some other periodicals made offers to most of the

The Shelter, Caen, 1944
oil on gesso panel, about 12 x 18

Dead Germans, 1944
ink and wash drawing, about 12 x 18½

Normandy Village, 1944
oil on gesso panel, about 24 x 15

Military Necessity, 1944
oil on gesso panel, 20 x 16

civilian artists in the units scattered over all the war theatres to continue their work for them. Howard Cook chose to accept an offer from *Collier's,* and I chose one from *Life.* If no other immediate change took place, I enjoyed the prestige of precise attachment to a famed magazine as war correspondent instead of to the anomalous government service in which I had worked.

I lost a race with Cook to bring our painted material to usable state in behalf of our rival magazines, but I followed him back home as quickly as I could. When *Life* in December, 1943, published one of its first big essays on the war illustrated in color by its far-flung artists, the piece, written by John Hersey and entitled "Experience by Battle," contained a solid collection of the paintings I had done on the invasion of Rendova.

After my return from the first tour of duty with the War Art Unit in the Pacific, I had to struggle mightily and with *Life's* help for the Chicago draft board's permission to make additional forays into the European theatre of war. For several years I continued working for *Life.* During that time, other series of my paintings were published, including those of war-torn London and Omaha Beach. Byron Thomas and I had jumped the scheduled gun, wangled a trip across the channel, and waded ashore on D plus 6 to see the big second front for ourselves. We had been roundly berated by the London office of *Life* on our return, but the New York people seemed delighted to use Thomas' good diary-type drawings of the adventure and my set of gouaches on this early aspect of the war in France. Later *Life* published my paintings of the penetration into Normandy and finally some of the work reflecting the winter war when I was attached to the Third Army on its entry into Germany.

Not all the paintings done during the heated immediacy of war are ones I can be proud of, apart from their possible historical usefulness. In some of my better moments of

Steep Street, Noumea, 1946
gouache, about 14 x 20

Low Tide, Barfleur, 1946
gouache, about 15 x 19

Captain Cook in New Caledonia, 1946
gouache, about 14 x 21

looking back I can, I think, extract the comfort of content with a small number of the things that spoke of the conflict in universal terms and that by a lucky miracle were able to stand on their own as reasonably meritorious painting. The perhaps hundred or so paintings and drawings I did both for the U.S. Engineers and for *Life* are now part of a collection of some thousand pictures displayed in a public gallery at the Pentagon.

In addition to the privilege of being able to paint the war when there was no contesting subject that had anywhere near this dramatic power, I count it as gain that I was able to be near some of the interesting military movers like General Patton and some of the writers and artists who were so close to the pulse of the conflict. Memories of correspondent camps in Europe are now blurred for me. Of course, I remember having a discussion with Ernest Hemingway, who visited our camp, about his little old aunt I had known in Carbondale, but what was said on both sides after that is forgotten. The vividness, however, of some of the experiences I shared with Robert Cromie, who left his sports-writing assignment on the Chicago *Tribune* to bring the readers of his paper knowledge of what the war was like and how their young Chicago neighbors in the army were faring in it, can never be forgotten. Tagging along with the unbelievably intrepid Cromie and usually with one other correspondent to make up a jeepload complement, I was often enough in the thick of the kind of activity which I would not have had the courage to encounter alone and which gave me some vital painting material.

On my re-establishment in Chicago when the war in Europe was over, I worked up a long series of paintings based on war travel. Places in the Pacific and in Europe to which I would otherwise have had no access were the settings for these pictorial by-products of the war. While the scars of war were apparent in some of the works, these were not essentially war paintings. They served to absorb the impulse for the exotic which I imagine is part of the craving of most artists. I was enabled here to match notes on the places I knew best with visions of lesser known and perhaps imperfectly understood places.

Daniel Longwell of *Life* magazine visited me in Chicago and inspected the large old house on the south side in which I had carved out a good third-story studio. He proposed that

Artist in Luxembourg, 1948
oil, 27 x 36

Book Shop, Paris, 1946
oil, 16 x 20

16th Street Markets, Chicago, 1947
gouache, 14 x 19

the magazine foot some of the bill by employing me, as reward for my war services, to re-examine the city with an eye freshened by the sights of war. For about a year I delighted in this labor of love, though only one painting I did in the extensive series ever saw the light of publication. This was a double-page spread on the beach at Oak Street.

Paris Book Stalls, 1947
oil, 12 x 16

John Steuart Curry died in 1946, ten years after the start of his residency at the University of Wisconsin. A two-man committee, the social scientists Professors Kolb and Barton, was appointed to find his successor. I learned they had set me down on their list of candidates. John Barton and his wife Rebecca came to look us over in Chicago. The tolerant nature of their glances did not seem to discourage additional investigation. Appointments of the special nature of this one are not made hurriedly, perhaps because in this appointment business first choices have to be granted time for refusal. As usual, I was irked by the delay and indecision. I reserve my patience only for my painting. In any case, after negotiations had been afoot for a long while, I still had time to make an extensive and leisurely sketching trip and appear with a one-man show in the Associated's Los Angeles gallery before a final decision to ask me to come to Madison was made in the summer of 1948.

While I had always looked with secret envy at Curry in his residency, I was still somewhat loath to leave my Chicago home. It contained everything needed for happy existence, and some fairly good painting had been produced there. There I could work in bathrobe and neglected beard for days at a time without fear of interruption. It was a place into which were born, satisfactorily, two additional offspring, my daughter Georgi and my son Neil. On the other hand, the advantages of the Wisconsin offer included a modest approach to financial support which might allow me to refuse some of the less entrancing commercial suggestions the gallery occasionally made. Except during infrequent and unreasonable mental states, I have never regretted the change.

Since I was primarily a "place" painter, in starting my work in Wisconsin I felt it would be expected that I look

Arizona Landscape, 1949
oil, about 16 x 20

Shakerag Street, ca. 1952
oil, 18 x 24

Wisconsin Swamp, ca. 1951
oil, 24 x 32

Juarez, 1948
oil, 20 x 16

well at the state's countryside. This was my own inclination in the fall of 1948. Until much of the material that I had sketched out West was exhausted, I alternated that material with Wisconsin subject matter. Then I plunged into an extensive investigation of Wisconsin's beauty. I think I still chose material that put ruggedness and maybe bittersweet sadness above scenic beauty. The towns, villages, and the Wisconsin countryside offered inexhaustible material for the artist.

John Curry and John Barton had set up a tentative framework for the encouragement of expression by the amateur rural painter. Barton in his book, *Rural Artists of Wisconsin,* related stories of some thirty young and old amateurs who had been discovered and helped by Curry. After my arrival in the state, I came to know some of these and many others who in a simple, open-hearted way were producing fresh and highly creditable works. James Schwalbach had taken the loosely set up Rural Art Project and, as a service of the College of Agriculture and the Extension Division, brought it to a fine state of precise organization. Regional art exhibits sparked by one-day art schools where criticisms and demonstrations were offered, together with the annual competitive exhibitions, created a worthy, unique, though unprofessional, art movement in Wisconsin.

In the early years of my residency I visited many of the regional exhibitions and criticized the works of hundreds of these rural painters. I never failed to marvel at the demonstration of simple love for painting and at the hunger of these artists for improvement. On my sketch trips through

The Bird House, ca. 1952
oil, 24 x 18

Wisconsin Barn, ca. 1952
oil, 16 x 20

the state I entered the homes of many of the artists and many, in turn, came to see me in my studio.

While I have had no classes to teach on the Wisconsin campus, many classes and groups have visited my studio and have elicited from me soul-searching testament as to what I am up to in my work. From all over the state have come busloads of apparently interested visitors, curious to see how a professional artist sets up his shop. And they have come to learn at first hand why abstract painting, if it will not meet its doom *this* year, will surely not survive the next. Though my studio is always open to the student visitor, it is only the occasional eager young art student with enough self-confidence to wrestle with an alternative point of view who becomes a regular visitor. I have found that most of my individual student callers come from sectors of the university outside the art areas. Though the interruptions sound extensive, and sometimes come at awkward moments, I have never seriously lacked the time for as much painting as I have the energy to complete.

In 1950, when F. Carlton Ball was on campus to organize a full-scale ceramic department, he invited faculty members to try their hands in the clay he found so enthralling. Tentatively, when it developed that all my pots collapsed after they attained a proud three-inch height, and then in a more intensive way, Ball and I started a collaboration which continued for some seven years. When he left Wisconsin, I joined him frequently for one- and two-week periods at my old Carbondale school, which had become the sizable Southern Illinois University. Roughly we divided our labors into his throwing of the pot, my application of decorative elements, and a mutual consideration of the glaze process. We produced perhaps four or five hundred works under our combined signatures. When not actually involved in physical pottery making, I covered hundreds of sketchbook pages with potential pottery ideas. In pottery, where the central purpose is to produce a beautiful object which may or may not be useful at the same time, there may be a natural utilization of fantasy and abstract pattern.

Pagan Magic, ca. 1954
cloth fabric produced by the Riverdale Co.

Bowl, "Europa," ca. 1955
stoneware pottery, diameter about 12 inches

Unglazed Pot, ca. 1956
bisque pottery, about 20 inches high

Painting, I believe, should always reflect and comment on life. If it were otherwise, the painting would be only a decorative object — like a pot, a rug, or a drape — one designed to serve and to look well. The artist's complex nature, which usually finds him brooding over a hotbed of conflicting impulses, was in my case sorted out by the ability to siphon off notions of a certain kind of design fantasy. My painting, then, could retain what I felt was unadulterated and reflective visual form.

Out of my interest in pottery came the discovery that the flow of fantasy could find outlet in other decorative areas. Associated American Artists had several projects going where the artist furnished designs that were converted into fabrics for draperies and other uses. These were amusing to work out. Several of the fabrics I designed were actually produced and proved to be very rewarding economically and not too disgracing aesthetically. Wallpaper was another area that could be played with creatively, though from my single venture into this field not enough came to finance the papering of our *own* kitchen.

Immersed as I was in the academic atmosphere, I was made conscious of the activity of the artist-teacher. I had known Santos Zingale and Alfred Sessler of the university staff for some years before I came to Wisconsin. Their paths as Milwaukee artists and mine as a Chicago artist had crossed many times in old Artist Union days when the government was practically the sole employer of the artist. As I observed their work as teachers, I envied them the rapport

Jackson Square, New Orleans, ca. 1953
mixed medium, about 11 x 13

they established with the young. I sometimes longed for the official capacity which would allow me to make suggestions to talented students with the reasonable expectation that the suggestions would be considered seriously. I had had brief flings with the teaching profession at the Chicago Art Institute and at Southern Illinois. I enjoyed this for a time, although I sensed that a prolongation of the periods involved would have been personally enervating. Although a couple of very short summer workshops primarily for rural painters were put in my care at Wisconsin, most of my subsequent teaching took place on other campuses. Several summer terms at Ohio University, Ball State Teachers' College, and Northern Michigan University in Marquette more than satisfied my urge. I thought I might have something to convey to students, but my desire to undertake formal teaching always dissipated quickly. I felt I was not suited to the extended and constant cooperative effort required to induce lasting progress in a student. Though I am always ready to share my painting experience with whoever might apply, selfishly I consider my own painting to be my prime reason for being. That the energies required for it might not be diluted, I decided to shun the classroom as a scene of regular activity.

In the first five years of my Wisconsin residency my painting took several twists and mild turns. I had made many rather finished pen-and-ink sketches during an extended stay in Door County, on trips to Bayfield and Ashland, and out of the state in New Orleans. Using these sketches, I became involved in a kind of small-scale, mixed-medium work. Usually the ink drawing served its prime purpose as offering the information for an organized work in gouache or oil. I now tried extending the drawing to serve as a second work in its own right. Wax crayons were applied in varying degrees of intensity over the inked lines. Washes of colored inks and watercolor applied over the surface penetrated or recoiled according to the degree of wax application. The result had a kind of luminosity not

Cornucopia, Wisconsin, ca. 1953
oil, 16 x 20

Boats and Floats, 1953
oil, 18 x 24

given to built-up pigment. Because of the flurried textural nature of the medium, compositional elements had to be simplified if the forms were to remain readable. When this compositional approach was carried over into larger, more complete paintings, I realized I was falling more and more into work motivated by arbitrary design. A sky pattern, for instance, would often contain a gerrymandered shape rung in for compositional value, overcoming the prime intention of cloud forms.

An interest in the medium of encaustic followed. The nonplasticity of wax-impregnated pigment made impossible the modelling of form to any degree of subtlety. This lack was compensated for by the unforeseen accidents peculiar to the medium. I fought forms down onto the panel and applied an alcohol torch flame to the face of the work. Pigment swimming in the wax base took on all kinds of textural beauty over which I had almost no control. The finished painting, rubbed to a gloss, usually emitted a jewel-like glow. If the result were good — and it most often was — the merit usually lay in the inherent nicety of the encaustic medium.

In 1953 my family and I spent a summer in Marquette, Michigan, while I undertook the teaching of a five-week summer session at the university there. The painting subjects that I found most intriguing were the rugged Lake Superior shore with dramatic boulders emerging from the cold blue waters. When I returned to Madison with a few

Rocks, Lake Superior, 1953
pen and ink, 11 x 13⅝

Rocks, Lake Superior, 1953
encaustic, 20 x 27

Rocks, Lake Superior, 1953
oil, about 14 x 18

finished gouaches and a sketchbook full of rocky landscape notes, the first problem I undertook was the trans-
lation of one of my detailed drawings into a respectably
sized encaustic painting. As I looked at the blurred, in-
distinct depiction I felt I had missed the quality of in-
cisiveness the sketch had suggested. I decided to refer
again to my drawing and to produce this time a smaller
work in oil, but one which would more nearly express the
intricacies of the craggy clump of landscape. To aid my
work I picked up little pebbles and stones which, while
held in the left hand, served as models to stand for the
large boulders and rocks constituting the materials of the
piece. Delving into the stone's character, examining its
pits and depressions, outgrowths and protrusions, its
subtle color nuances, its veins and its fissures, I experi-
enced a way of seeing that had never occurred to me before.

In the past I had set up for reference the materials for
an occasional still life. I had also once in a while referred
to a solid natural object for clues to a painting's detail.
These, however, were usually freely brushed responses to
the material I was observing. In my rock landscape I almost rebuilt the rock, analyzing what it was that visually
made it a rock and finding a way to make over on a two-
dimensional surface the essence and feel of the object. I

Mellow Objects, 1953
oil, 20 x 16

Magic Realism, 1953
oil, 12 x 16

am sure I cannot convince many that this was a tremendous discovery. But to me the experience was new and exciting.

After the rock painting was completed it occurred to me that still-life compositions pre-arranged as completely as possible in the form of spatial models of varied materials and textures might serve to complement the rocky landscape as alternatives in all-out form investigation. My mind had not yet opened to an easy flow of ideas in the still-life vein and I cast about for a suitable subject or collection of objects. I remembered seeing some interesting magician's paraphernalia in the home of a neighbor. The amateur magician, Art Brush, fell in with my plans and made available his whole bag of tricks, from which I selected some objects. The painting which emerged, "Magic Realism," still did not achieve the every-last-cell-of-matter effect I was after because I had shrunk the material down. The reduced scale made it impossible to work up to a potential of full-form development.

I decided on further experimentation and came up with another theme which this time made sense in the harmonious relationship of well-weathered materials. The painting, called "Mellow Objects," contained a violin which also had to be reduced in scale so that it could be cramped into the moderate format I made available, with an attendant diminution in scale of the other objects. For the first time I used the well-known trompe l'oeil device of a frontal plane with shallow depth.

It was not until I did "A Lincoln Portrait" that I established the idea of painting all the elements in my works in almost exactly the same scale as the objects themselves. Always, though, I have allowed myself liberties so that reduction, enlargement, or other distortions are parts of the flexible means I employ whenever necessary.

In 1954 I embarked on what I thought would be a short series of severely executed still-life paintings that would make an interesting departure from the kind of painting I had considered my life work. But for the past ten years I have not been able to tear myself away from the expression that has obsessed me. Except for my drawing and an occasional finger-warming exercise in alternate media to determine whether I can still work that way, I cannot seriously conceive of discontinuing something I find so entrancing. Far from running dry, I find that there is a constant clamor of ideas seeking outlet. Nor is this in the form of putting the pipe on the right and the bowl on the left one time, and then alternately coming up with the bowl on the right and the pipe on the left side of a composition. Countless subjects are possible when objects are used symbolically.

Sometimes I have been asked to explain how my painting ideas emerge. It would be pompous to talk in terms of flashes of revelation. What directs inspiration to the churning mind would be impossible to determine. I can only say that inventive flow of thought feeds on itself, that the harder one works to bring his visions to fruition the more eagerly additional ideas crowd the mind to supplant the expended idea.

I try to keep myself surrounded with objects that may be curious or ordinary, intrinsically beautiful or ugly. These are found, purchased, borrowed, or given to me by people who find themselves incapable of discarding an unvaluable chunk of curiosa in a refuse barrel. In this connection I have tramped through city dumps and junkyards picking up occasional slabs of weathered and paint-crackled wood to serve as background onto which I might fasten the materials for a speculative still life. Thus, too, I have found and cherished other twisted and broken things that conceivably might evoke an idea. While once I was wont to sketch the outsides of antique shops and second-hand stores, I now explore their interiors. I may have an object in daily view for several years before the acquisition of a relating object sets off a train of thought resulting in a picture idea. Visiting a class that John Rogers, a former university student, was teaching in Eau Claire, I noticed and was given a battered head dummy

Queen of Kings, page 265

Everyman, page 177

Soliloquy, page 107

In Sea and Fire, in Earth,
in Air, page 237

Of Many Things, page 145

which in the 1920's had probably shone bright in a milliner's window supporting an Empress Eugenie hat. It was used in the classroom in the way plaster casts once served for preliminary head study. This object lay on my shelves for several months. Then knowledge of a much-discussed motion picture penetrated my consciousness. Borrowing an ancient Egyptian copper bowl, I created a Cleopatra theme using the poor dummy head as heroine. Attended by other appropriate notes, the painting emerged as "Queen of Kings."

Sometimes a painting stems from a reverse order of thinking. The idea having struck, first procedure resembles the action of a casting director who weighs the merits of available actors as candidates for the required performance. Having thought of the theme for a painting I could call "Everyman," I pondered the generic objects that might serve as symbols to enact my tableau. Rummaging in the attic of the Wisconsin Historical Society Museum resulted in loans that allowed me to employ a gold-headed cane for the "rich man," an old stethoscope for the "doctor," a scratched tin cup for the "beggarman," and so on through the component list. Several times I have used the child's rebus idea of stating my symbols in the form of a left-to-right reading. In this way "Soliloquy" and "In Sea and Fire, in Earth, in Air" were constructed. "Of Many Things," in a variation of the idea, stretches out the Lewis Carroll items that end on the right with cabbages and kings.

Symbolism does not always motivate these compositions. There are times when color harmony or textural contrasts set off notions of compositional thought. Always, however, I have demanded from myself a core of meaning. This may be obvious, or conversely so subtle that I cannot myself be certain of all the implications involved. It is embarrassing and dangerous for the artist to be too explicit verbally about his endeavor. I would be very reluctant to put my finger on every last element in one of my paintings and justify its use by scoring its intention. The model in this sense is Picasso, to whom nobody has the temerity to apply for meaning. It is known that he will just smile and shrug his shoulders. The envied mantle of profundity naturally encloaks such enigmatic characters.

I once wrote about one level of my painting that I demand "expression within a realistic framework, with the

Photo by Archie Lieberman

reality carried to so intense a degree that it becomes almost fantasy, and a subject painted with such unashamed skill that a conviction of truth evokes beauty." While the clear ingredients for speculation are always present in my paintings, how they are put together, or whether meaning can be extracted at all from them, varies considerably with the character and degree of sympathy of the spectator. Apart from the obvious or elusive meanings in my work, I would hopefully wish the sympathetic spectator to respond to a pleasure-giving quality in a painting.

Once I credited the persistence of my efforts in meticulously worked still life to a desire to demonstrate aesthetic worth in a form at the opposite pole from the abstraction that was almost officially designated as the way the artist should be working in the middle of the twentieth century. The protest aspects of this intention have long since evaporated. They have been replaced by a genuine love for, and a passionate involvement in, this way of expression.

In beginning the actual painting, I establish my subject by making an almost diagrammatic map of my materials, roughly brushing them in. When I have the composition fairly well set, I spend weeks painting and scraping, nurturing and tickling my forms along with small, short-lived brushes, working toward closer and closer realization of substance. My methods require a slow, careful creeping up on the finished painting. Sometimes what seem suitable and workable material arrangements will not translate well onto my gesso panel. I must hold myself flexible and be willing to change my materials or arrangements throughout the process of painting. Each object and each new arrangement seems to demand a different process of development. I have never come to a set system. Perhaps that is why the actual painting remains a challenge to me. When I succeed, the objects in my painting seem to come to a life of their own.

I have never been frightened by the bogey of detail. When detail is integrated into a total scheme, it can only serve to enrich the result. Dostoyevsky said that he could see the universe in a square foot, and William Blake "a world in a grain of sand." Nor have I been constrained by the cliché insisting that a painter leave things to the spectator's imagination to the point of requiring him to complete a vaguely suggested form or to read meaning into works that contain none. In any good painting there is plenty for sensitive people to ponder without asking them to complete, mentally, the artist's intentions about form.

While the mistaken designation of my work as trompe l'oeil is not of earth-shaking consequence and while I cannot deny that elements of this classic idiom are present in my work, my chief intention is not merely to push reality so far as to fool the eye into believing that it is observing tangible, three-dimensional material. Aesthetic exploration of surface and of substance, the statement-making presentation of meaningful subject matter, and the achievement of plain beautiful painting all take precedence over the business of eye befuddlement. I avoid many of the technical means of accentuating the effects so typical of this genre. While I admire sensitive trompe l'oeil painters ranging from the seventeenth-century Dutch to the nineteenth-century Americans like Harnett and Peto, I do not want to follow them into their illusory world.

Many critics have today become apprehensive of skillful, meticulously realized painting. They are still reacting against the days of the French Salon when the Academy ruled with an iron fist. Fearful that concern for technical proficiency might deny wall space to a Manet or a Cézanne while granting it to vastly inferior talents, they are predisposed to accept those manifestations of art they feel to be novel or fresh, even though technical execution may be feeble. Critics seem eager to express appreciation of any meaningless but excitingly put down blob of pigment if nobody has thought to put down the blob in just that way before. They can find originality and strong talent in collages of clipped-out, designer-arranged, and pasted-down magazine reproductions and other patches of raw material, but they often do not know what to make of an artist who with brush, paint, hand, eye, and heart alone brings to the point of tingling reality an interpretation of the world around him.

For many years I have hopefully been prophesying the decline of abstract painting. Perhaps by the time this book is published these works will have taken on an unfashionable, outworn look. The new enthusiasm, Pop Art, while it is at least *about* something, cannot, I believe, hold sway long. Its current success is attributable to the fact that it has provided a welcome alternative to abstract painting, which has become a burden even to its most devoted admirers. The studied crudity of Pop Art will cause

an inevitable revulsion to set in fairly soon. Op Art, with its eye-stimulating dazzle, is an interesting combination of science and art, but here unfortunately science far outweighs art. Other schools of art will come and will go. Somehow there will, I trust, always be room for works of reality reflecting contemporary existence and holding interest for people who think of art as something more enduring than a passing fashion show.

Several magazine editors have envisioned institutional use for my current mood of work. Over the years I created for *Time* a small number of paintings that were used as covers on the magazine. Several of the paintings gave me the opportunity to work in the characteristic still life I enjoy doing. For *Look* magazine, with the sympathetic and knowledgeable collaboration of Allen Hurlburt, its art director, I gloried in a three- or four-year project which allowed me to undertake a fourteen-picture series of still-life works, each of which symbolized one of America's principal religions. For Eli Lilly and Company, I executed a seven-piece series of still-life works that related to that number of medical disciplines. These latter series gave me opportunities to work along lines I might have chosen for myself if I had had normal access to the materials involved. As specific assignments, they presented no strain other than the mixed pleasure and pain inherent in the production of any of my other works.

Some of my friends tell me that still life has too constricted a scope. They urge me to move on to something else. I find I cannot agree. Of course, every form has its limits, but within these limits there is an infinite array of subjects on which to comment. I can comment on time and the world in which we live, on man as reflected by the things man makes and lives with, on life and on death. Physical changes or extraneous events may force a halt to these particular aesthetic proceedings. When my eyes fail and my feet flatten and my hand loses its steadiness, I will probably rationalize a reason for painting in another way. But ideas still abound. And since the required physical resources, though diminishing, are yet reliant, I hope I may be forgiven for saying there is still life in the old boy.

Aaron Bohrod

Madison, Wisconsin
July, 1965

A Decade of Still Life

facing, A Lincoln Portrait, 1954, 20 x 16

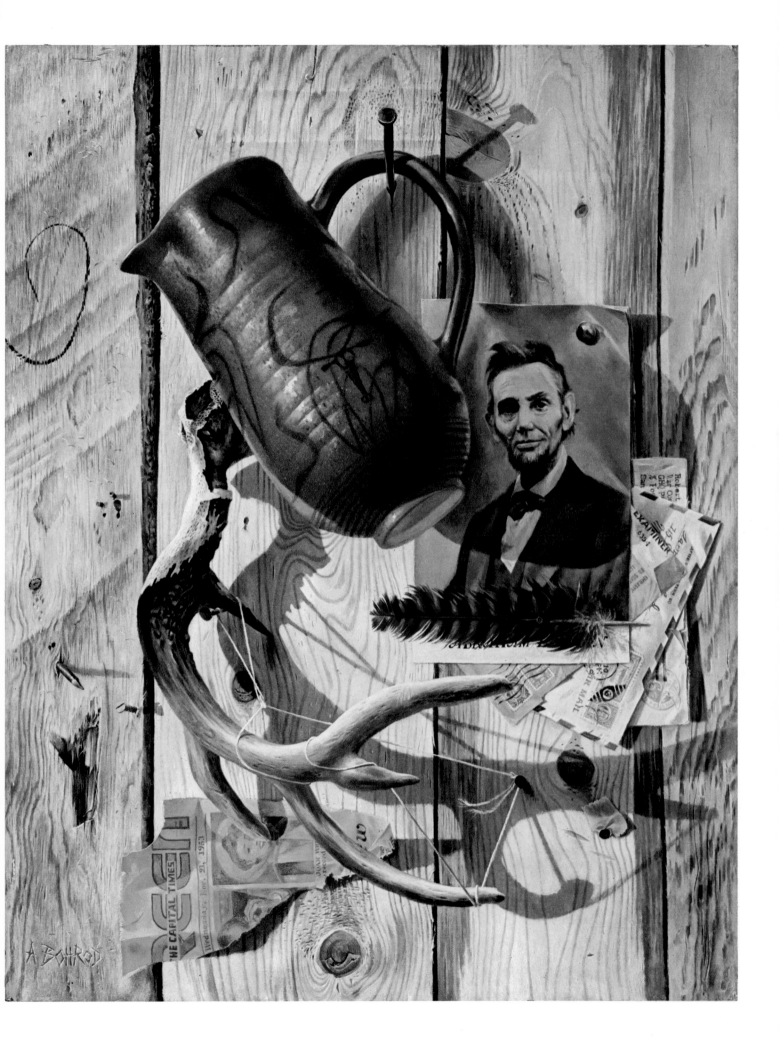

Peanuts, 1954, 5½ x 9

Popcorn, 1954, 5½ x 9

Objects on a Barrel, 1954, 24 x 18

Popcorn and Nude, 1954, 5½ x 9

Sea Things, 1954, 6 x 13

facing, Pillar, 1954, 30 x 18

The White Rose, 1954, 9 x 12

The Pacific, 1954, 12 x 16

Beauty and Beast, 1954, 12 x 9

October, 1954, 20 x 16

Banana, 1954, 5½ x 9

Anatomy Lesson, 1954, 9 x 12

Still Life with Pretty Girl, 1955, 16 x 12

facing, The New Venus, 1954, 16 x 12

Artifacts, etc., 1955, 12 x 16

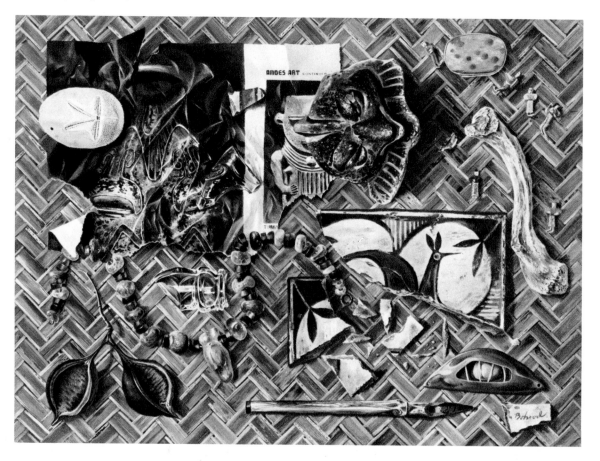

Playthings, 1954, 5 ½ x 9

facing, Africana, 1955, 16 x 12

Bird and Grapes, 1955, 5½ × 9

facing, Animal Kingdom, 1955, 16 × 20

Anthropology, 1955, 5⅝ x 9

Infinity, 1955, 5½ × 9

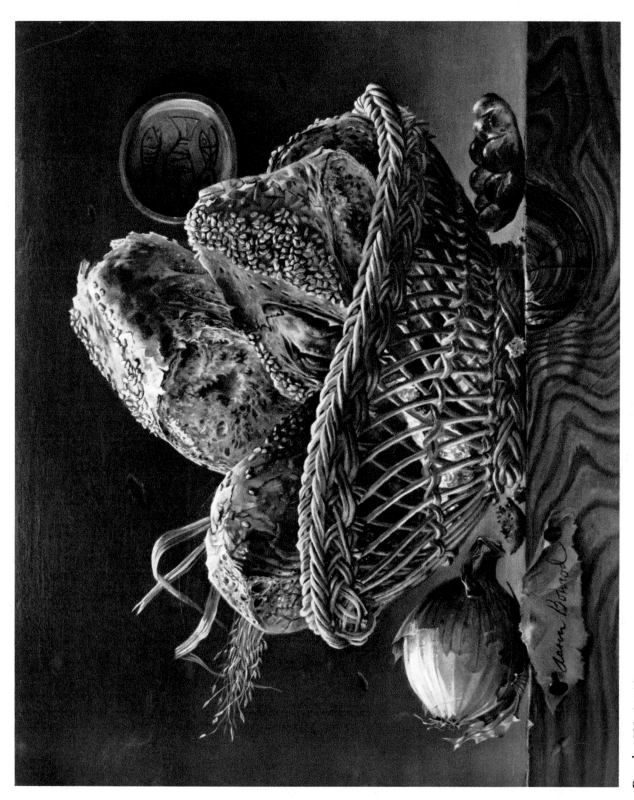

facing, Georgic, 1955, 18 x 24

Bread, 1955, 9 x 12

79

Still Life with Portraits, 1954, 24 x 32

Governor Knight, 1955, 16 x 12

facing, Horses, 1956, 13 x 10

The Rock, 1956, 16 x 12

The Lizard, 1956, 12 x 9

The Desert, 1956, 5¼ x 9

The Fortress, 1956, 5¼ x 9

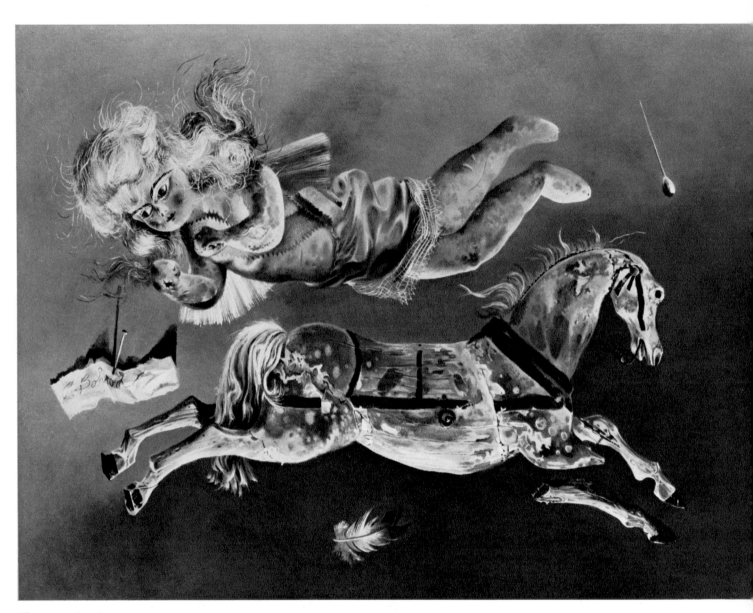

Toys, 1956, 9 x 12

facing, Objects on Birch Bark, 1955, 20 x 16

Uprooted, 1956, 20 x 16

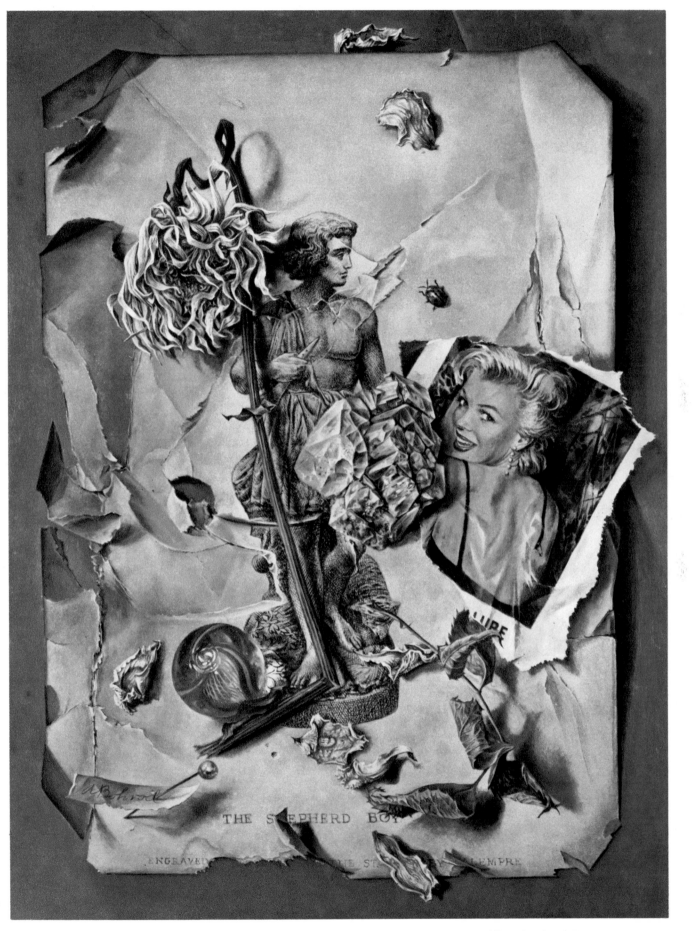

The Shepherd Boy, 1956, 12 x 9

Mother Earth, 1956, 12 x 16

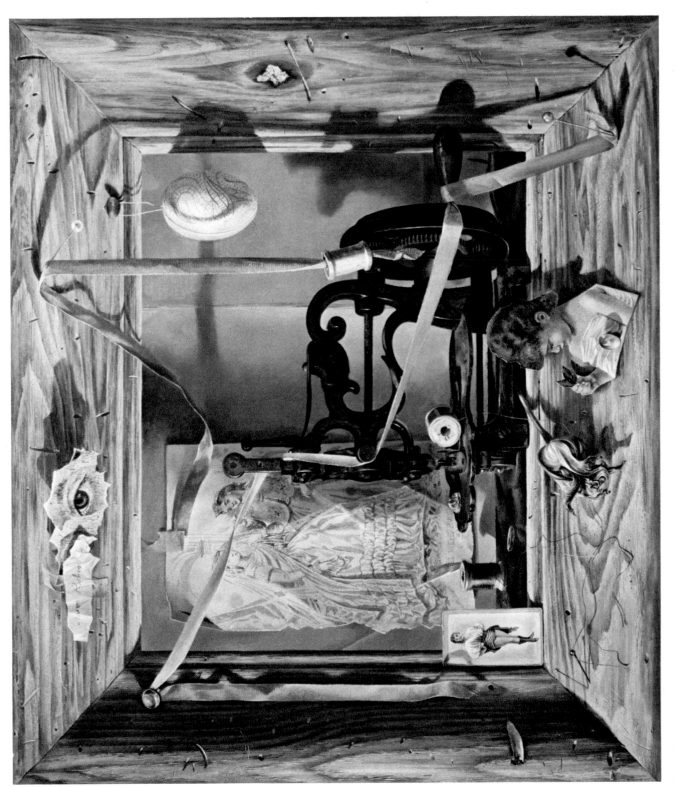

facing, Sacred and Profane, 1956, 9 x 12

The Women, 1956, 17 x 21

95

Victorian Blocks, 1956, 12 x 9

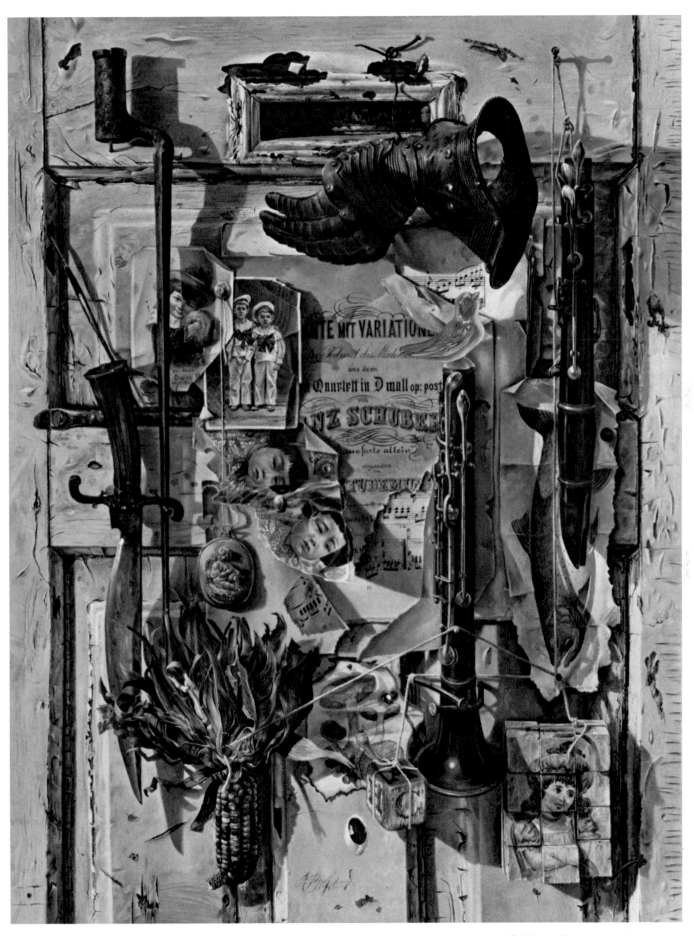

Of War and Peace, 1956, 32 x 24

Old Paint, 1955, 5½ x 9

Sugar and Spice, 1956, 9 x 12

Tree Swallow, 1956, 7½ x 9½

26001

Bird and Gauntlet, 1956, 12 x 24

101

Figurine, 1956, about 12 x 9

Yesterday, 1956, 24 x 16

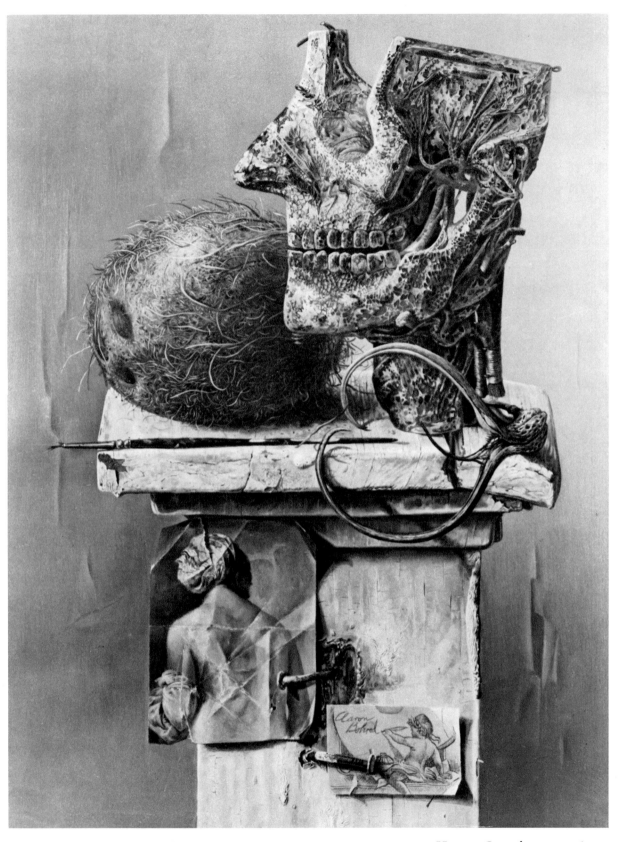

Human Comedy, 1957, 16 x 12

facing, Onions and Rose, 1957, 20 x 16

Decline and Fall, 1956, 8 x 24

facing, Soliloquy, 1956, 12 x 16

106

Things of This World, 1956, 10 x 24

facing, Bed of Leaves, 1956, 12 x 16

The Great Patriots, 1957, 12 x 9

Dead Sea Scrolls, 1957, 12 x 8½

Sparrow Hawk and Grapes, 1957, 24 x 7

Analytic Glance, 1957, 24 x 18

The Golden West, 1957, 12 x 16

Theodore Roosevelt, 1958, 15 x 11

A Row of Things, 1957, 7⅜ x 19⅝

facing, "Nevermore," 1957, 24 x 32

116

The Methodists, 1957, 24 x 18

The Roman Catholics, 1957, 16 x 12

Victorian Venus, 1957, 13 x 6⅛

Cupboard Door, 1957, 15¾ x 15¾

121

The Lutherans, 1957–58, 20 x 16

facing, The Mormons, 1957, 20 x 16

The Web, 1958, 20 x 8½

facing, Self Portrait (The Art of Painting), 1958, 12 x 9

The Jews, 1958, 20 x 16

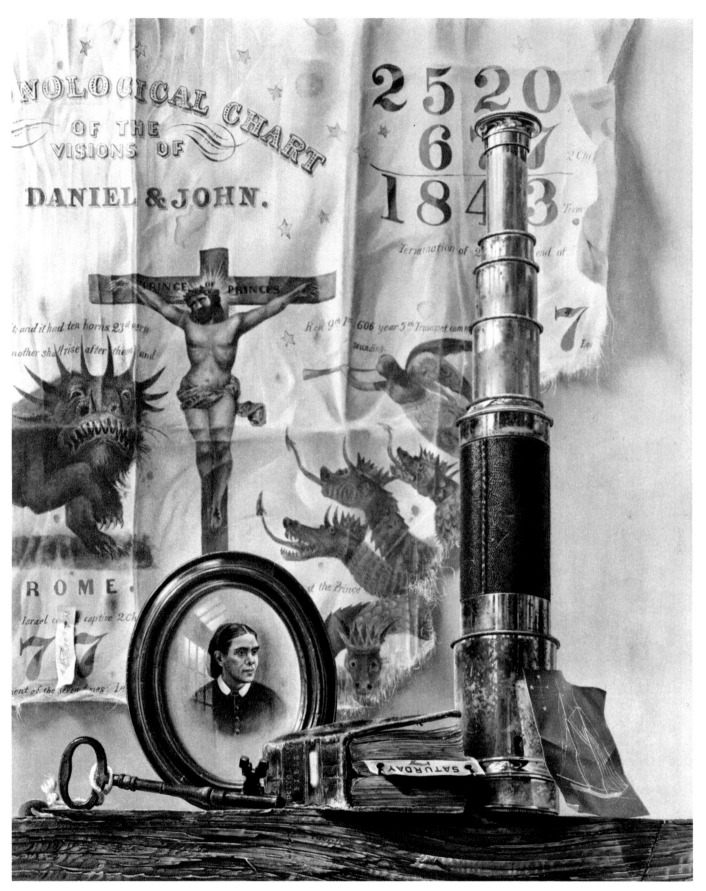

The Seventh Day Adventists, 1958, 20 x 16

Eve, 1958, 6⅛ x 9⅞

Red Onions, 1958, 16 x 20

129

Thrush and Mushroom, 1958, 8¼ x 6⅜

Decorations, 1958, 9 x 12

The Eye and I, 1958, 5¾ x 5¾

facing, Arrangement in Green and Gold, 1958, 24 x 18

The Baptists, 1958, 20 x 16

The Christian Scientists, 1958, 18 x 14

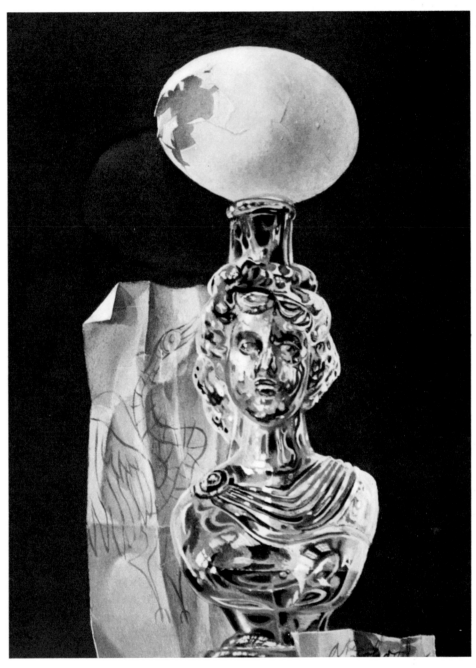

Leda, 1958, 6¾ x 5

facing, Still Life with Rembrandt, 1958, 24 x 14

Ivan Albright (Through a Glass Darkly), 1958, 14⅜ x 10⅞

Art and Nature, 1958, 12 x 9

Angel, 1958, 8½ x 6

facing, Night's Herald, 1958, 24 x 14

141

Eggplant and Bread Rolls, 1958, 9 x 11

facing, Lady Fair, 1958, 20 x 16

Europa, 1958, 12 x 16

facing, Of Many Things, 1958–59, 16 x 20

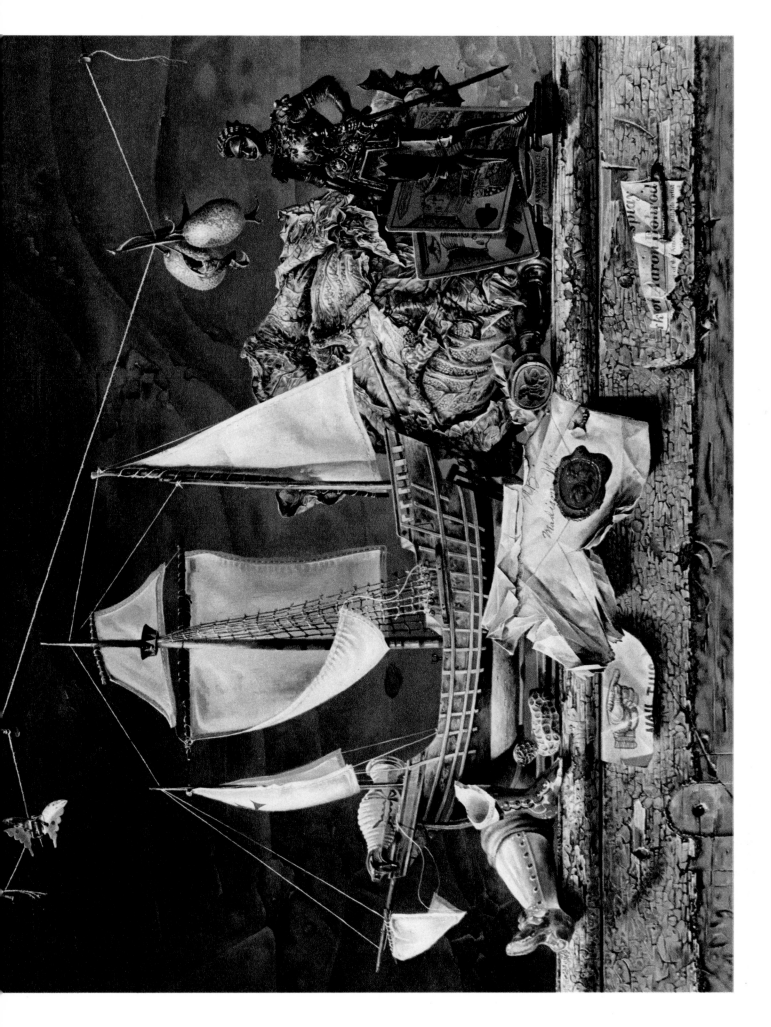

Hanging Pear, 1958, 9¼ x 6¾

Dancer, 1958, 8½ x 6½

Diana, 1959, 24 x 10

Harness Piece, 1959, 10 x 8

The Episcopalians, 1959, 20 x 16

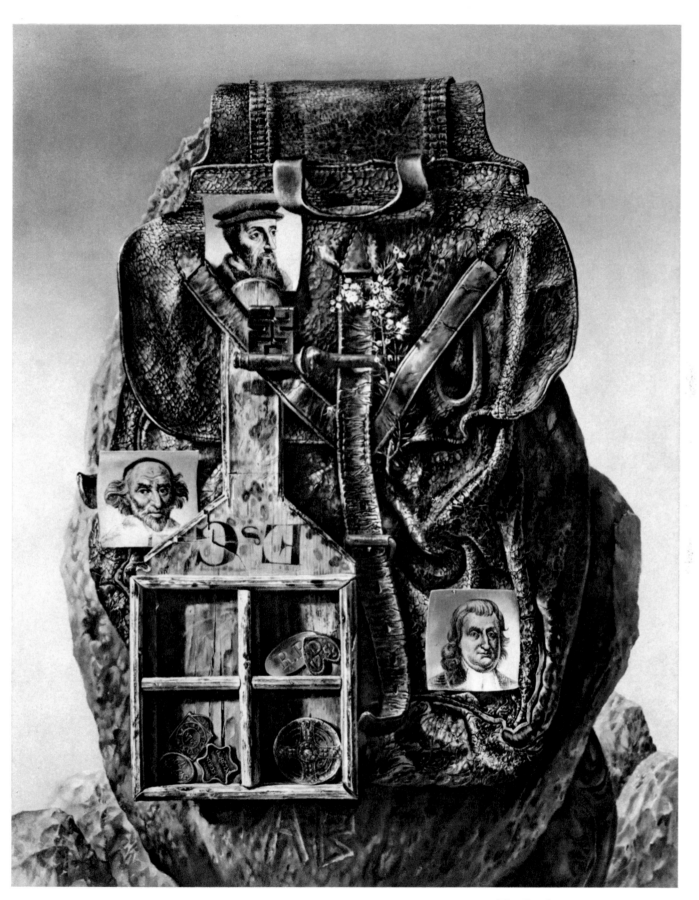

The Presbyterians, 1959, 20 x 16

Human Comedy II, 1959, 16 x 12

Oriental, 1959, 12 x 9

Still Life with Darwin, 1959, 8½ x 12

Twain, 1959, 5¾ x 9

The Shelf, 1959, 12 x 20

facing, Composition with Bottles, 1959, 9⅝ x 13¾

156

The Disciples of Christ, 1959, 20 x 16

The Congregationalists, 1959, 20 x 16

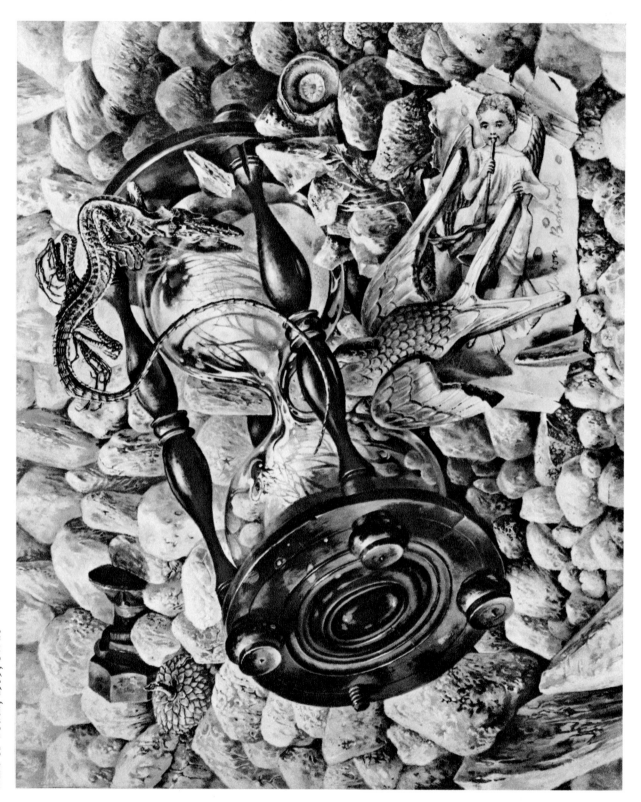

Bird of Youth, 1959, 8 x 10

facing, Prologue, 1959–60, 18 x 24

160

Cardiology, 1959, about 15 x 11

Pediatrics, 1960, 15⅝ x 12¾

Still Life with Old Shoe, 1959, 12½ x 16

facing, The Red Cabbage, 1959, 17¼ x 23¼

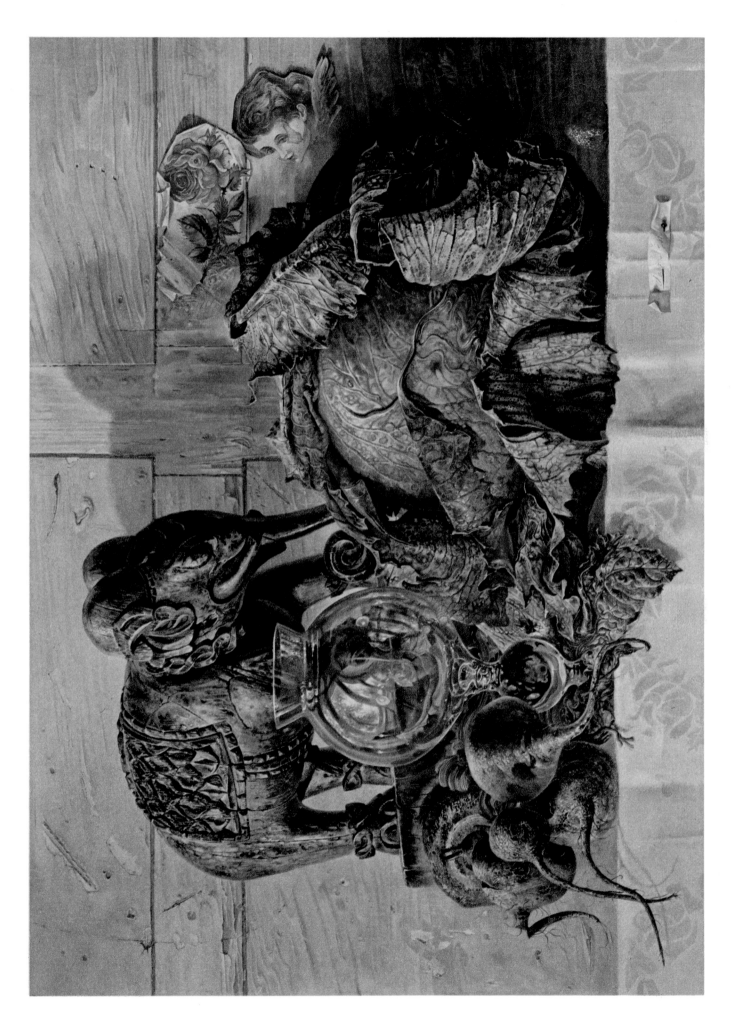

Reclining Figure, 1959, 20 x 16

facing, The Birds, 1960, 27¾ x 15½

167

Chestnuts, 1960, 6⅜ x 8¼

facing, Brief Candle, 1960, 32 x 24

169

The Quakers, 1959, 20 x 16

The Eastern Orthodox, 1960, 20 x 16

Infectious Disease, 1960, about 15 x 12

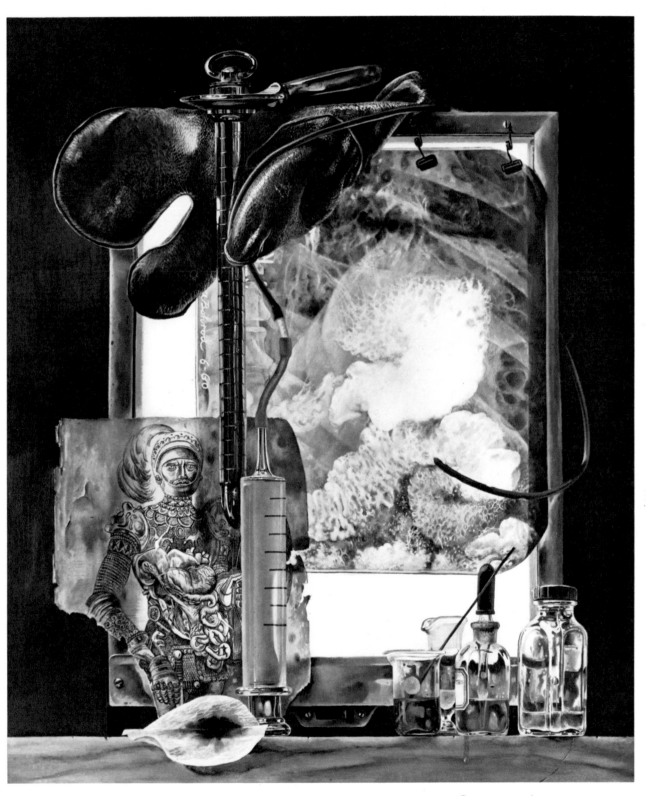

Gastroenterology, 1960, 22 x 18

Little Monkey, 1960, 10 x 8

Lady and Egg, 1960, 8¾ x 6¾

Arrangement in Black and White, 1960, 12 x 24

facing, Everyman, 1960, 24 x 32

Lot's Wife, 1960, 8¾ x 6¾

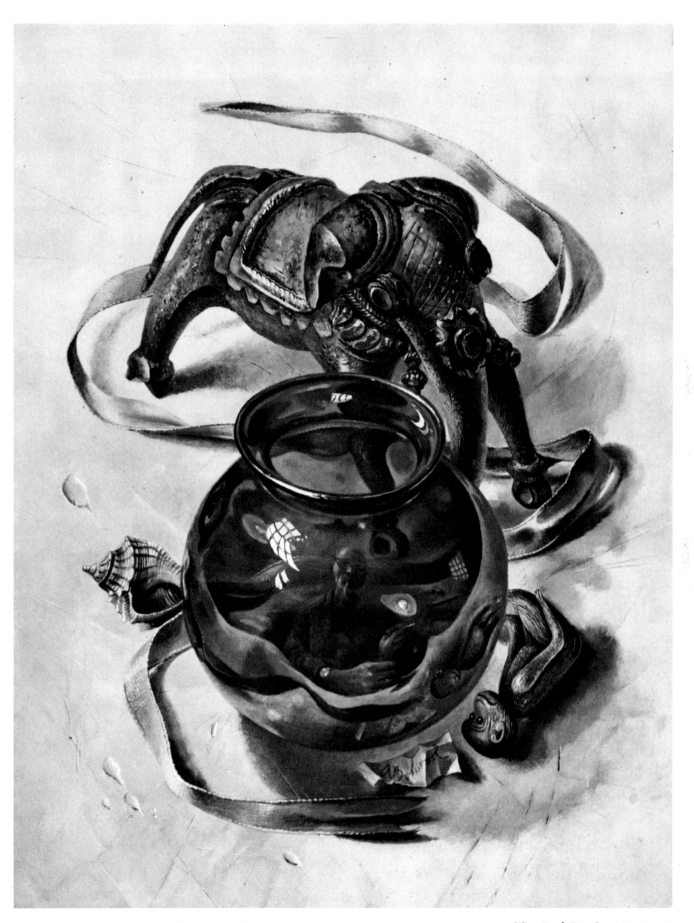

The Red Bowl, 1960, 12 x 9

Japanese Doll, 1960, 16 x 12

facing, Double Wedding, 1961, 16 x 12

Angelica, 1960, 16 x 12

Cycle, 1960, 20 x 16

Psychiatry-Neurology, 1960, 18¾ x 15¾

Salt and Water Metabolism, 1960, 15 x 12

The Horse, 1960, 16 x 20

186

Purple Ribbon and Blue Cow, 1960–61, 14 x 24

187

Jungle, 1960, 9 x 12

facing, Piece of Work, 1961–62, 24 x 19½

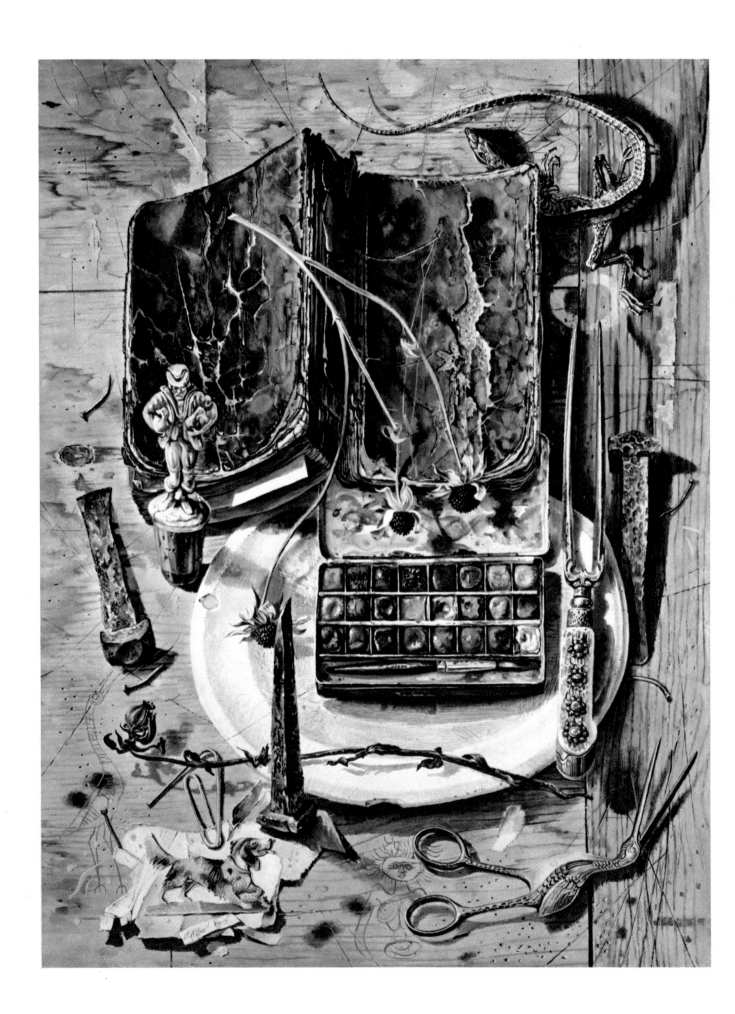

Corncob Pipe, 1961, 16 x 12

facing, The Watercolor Box, 1961, 16 x 12

American Eagle, 1961, 16 x 12

facing, Cyrano, 1962, 20 x 16

Ornaments, 1961, 12 x 16

Books and Beasts, 1961, 14½ x 20¼

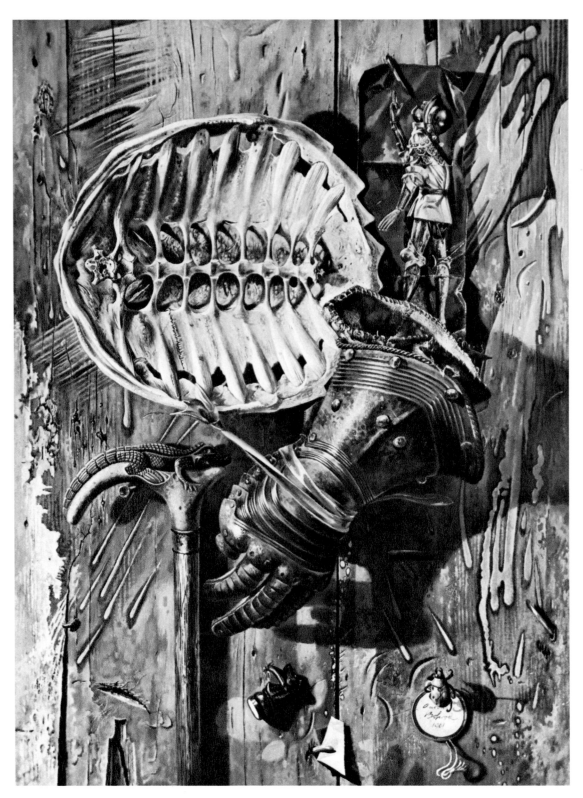

The Turtle Shell, 1961, 22 x 16

facing, Arrangement in Blue and Gray, 1961, 20 x 10

196

Paper Tiger, 1961, 9 x 6

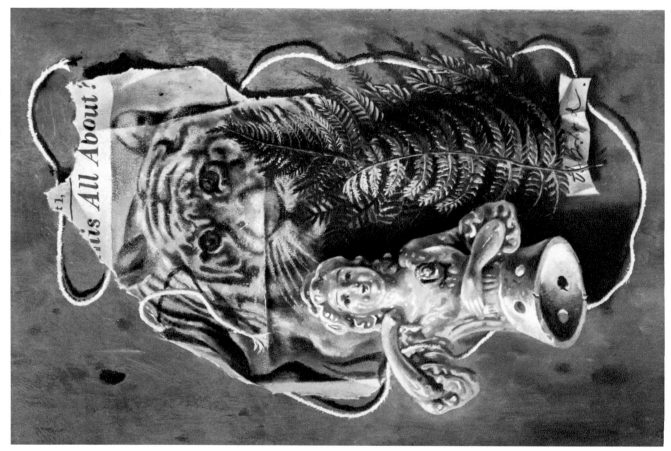

The Gift, 1961, 9 x 6

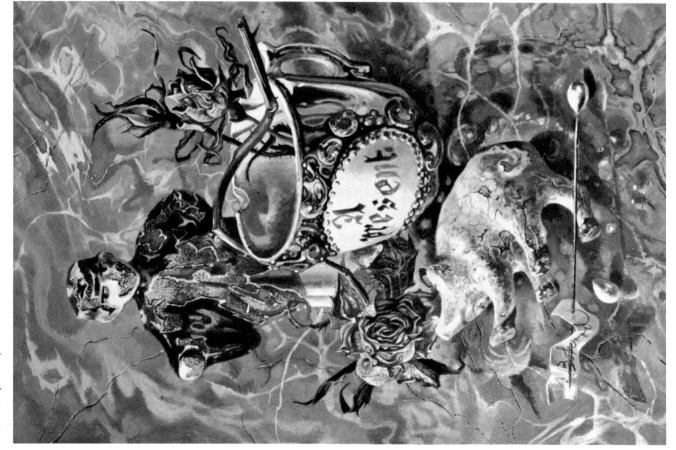

198

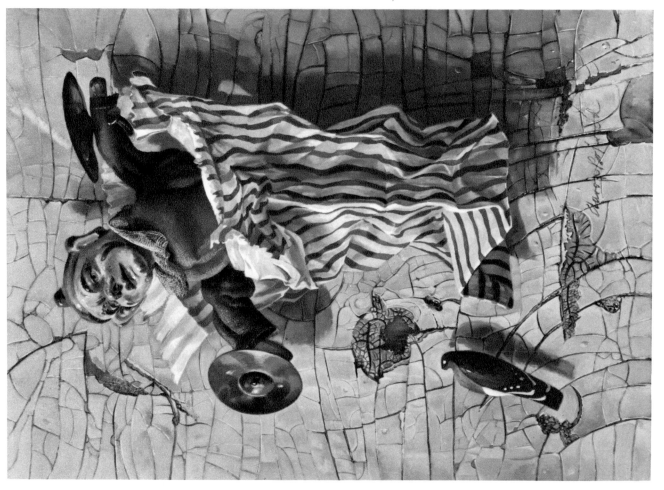

Clown Puppet, 1961, 11 x 8

The Hinge, 1961, 9½ x 7

The Retreats, 1961, 20 x 18

The Sea, 1961, 12 x 9

Flower and Fruit, 1961, 10 x 8

The Summer Session, 1961, 19 x 15

The Swallowtail, 1961, 6 x 10

Arrangement in Red and White, 1961, 12 x 16

Barong and Fish, 1961, 16 x 12

Pomona, 1961, 16 x 12

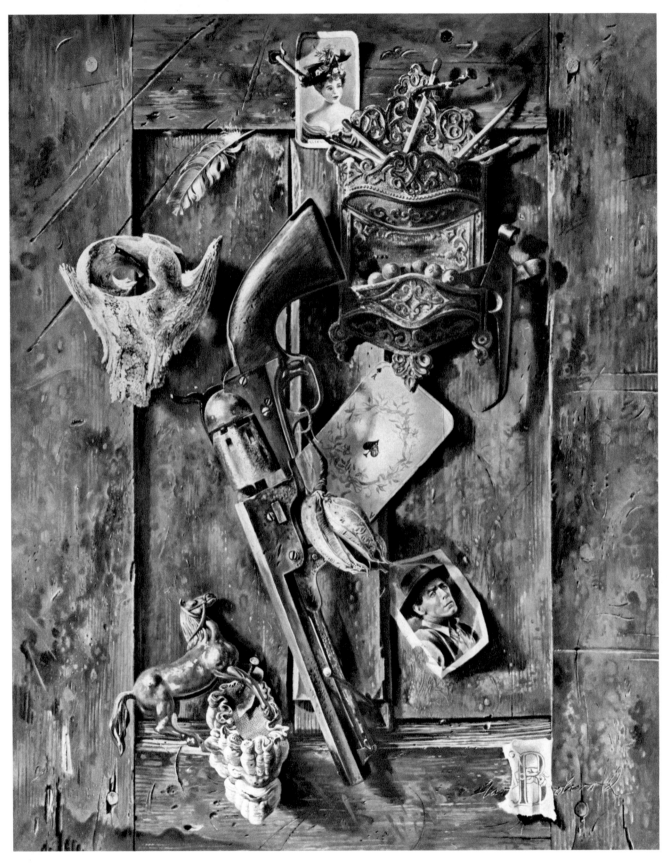

The Six Shooter, 1961, 20 x 16

facing, A Game of Pairs, 1962, 10 x 8

Grotesque, 1961, 20 x 12

The Shadow, 1961, 32 x 24

211

A Glass Menagerie, 1962, 12 x 24

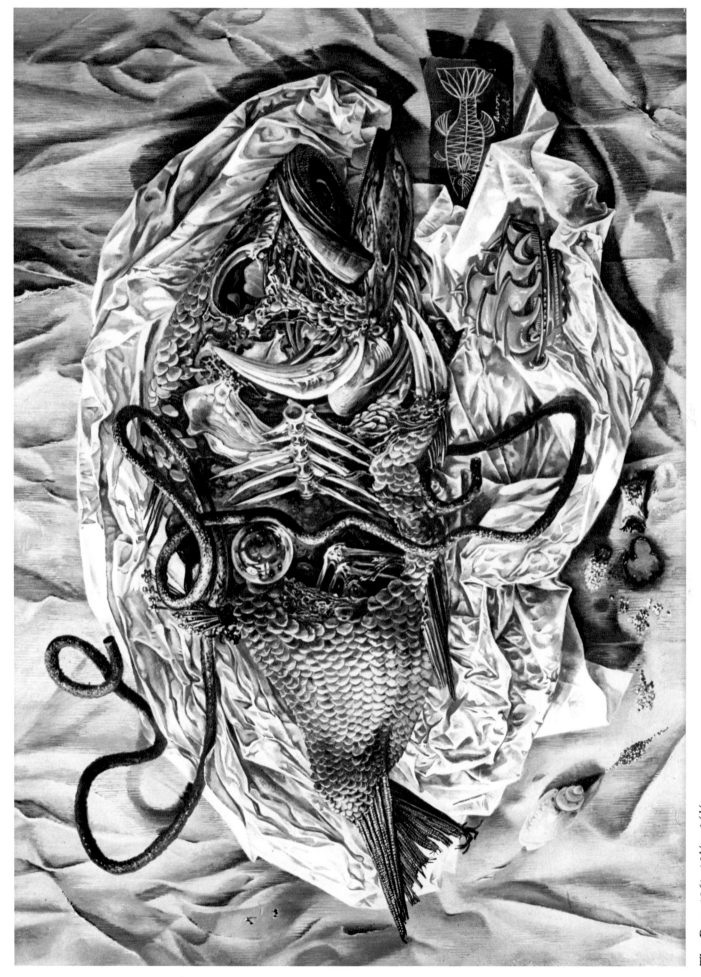

The Bass, 1961, 10½ x 14½

213

The Stage, 1961, 12 x 16

The Geographer, 1961, 12½ x 16½

Fallen Angel, 1961, 12 x 9

facing, Italian Boy, 1962, 10 x 8¼

217

218

Still Life with Cloth Rose, 1962, 7 x 5

facing, Gilded Angel, 1962, 16 x 12

Still Life with Melons, 1961, 14 x 24

Hub and Hals, 1962, 16⅜ x 22½

Chinese Lanterns and China Hands, 1962, 14 x 10

The Bonnet, 1962, 16 x 12

Sunflower and Raspberries, 1962, 10 x 12

facing, Of Form and Color, 1962, 20 x 16

Still Life with Paper Bird, 1962, 11¾ x 8¾

The Golden Apple, 1962, 16 x 12

Still Life with Paper Moon, 1962, 24 x 32

The Admiral, 1962, 18 x 24

Madame Van Eyck, 1962, 8¾ x 6⅝

Cylinder, Sphere, and Cone, 1962, 4⅛ x 9¼

230

By Any Other Name, 1962, 12 x 9

Slice of Life, 1962, 10 x 14

facing, Sere and Yellow, 1962, 16 x 20

232

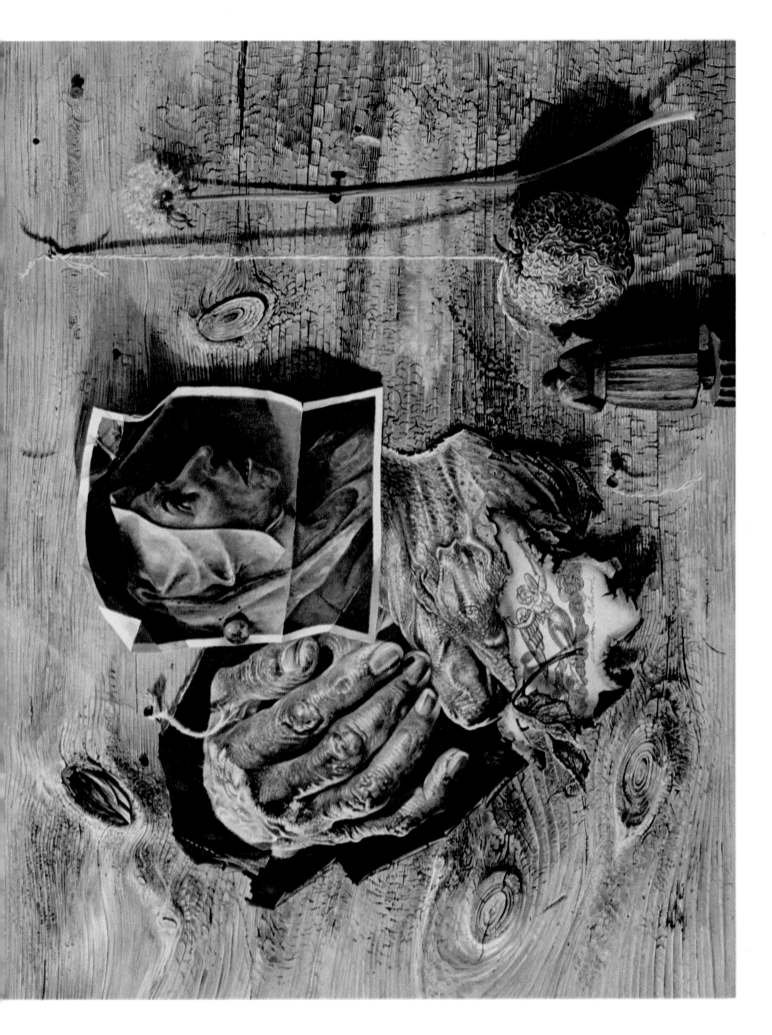

233

Sunflowers, 1962, 23½ x 17⅜

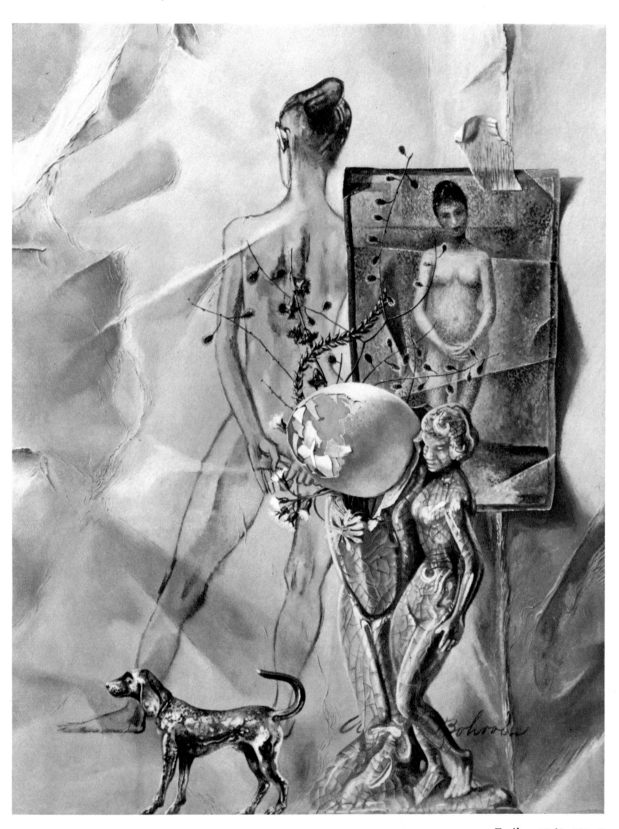

Frailty, 1962, 12 x 9

facing, Gulliver, 1962, 12 x 16

In Sea and Fire, in Earth, in Air, 1962, 14 x 24

237

"And Thou," 1962, 13⅞ x 20

Speaking of Money, 1962, 18 x 24

Blind Love, 1963, 10 x 8

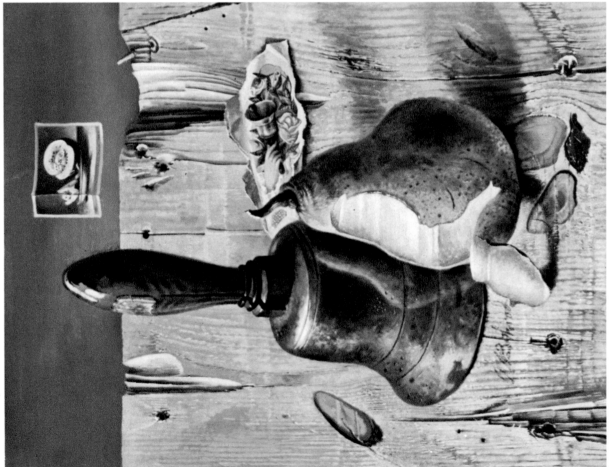

The Peale, 1962, 9 x 7

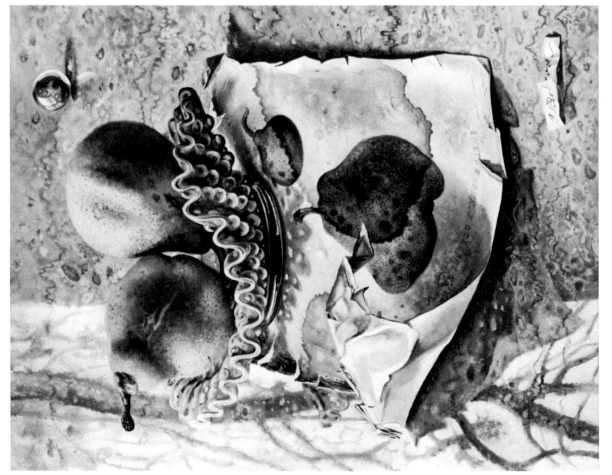

Two Pears, 1962, 12 x 9

241

Chrysanthemums, 1962, 14 x 10

facing, Pipe, Gun, Mug, Hals, 1962–63, 24 x 12

243

Pandora, 1963, 16 x 12

The Golden Pear, 1963, 16 x 12

Venus III, 1963, 6 x 10

facing, The Botticelli Venus, 1963, 16 x 20

246

Pietà, 1963, 24 x 18

The Renoir Venus, 1963, 16 x 12

The Sea Chest, 1963, 16 x 20

Lorelei, 1963, 12½ x 16½

The Portrait, 1962, 9 x 7

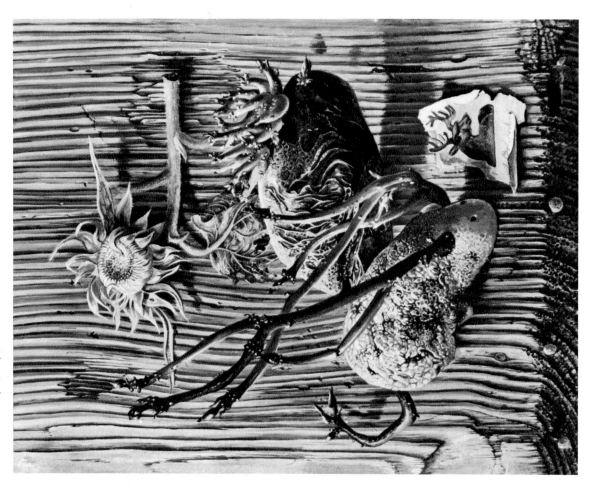

Potato Beasts, 1962, 9 x 7

252

The Sweet Life, 1963, 12 x 20

253

Sea Horses, 1963, 8 x 10

Song of the Sea, 1963, 9 x 12

The Letter, 1963, 11 x 8

facing, Carrousel, 1963, 14½ × 18½

The Flock, 1963, 12 × 16

The Laugh, 1963, 12 x 9

Quail, 1963, 10 x 8

Light of the East, 1963, 10 x 8

facing, Conrad A. Elvehjem, 1963, 16 x 12

261

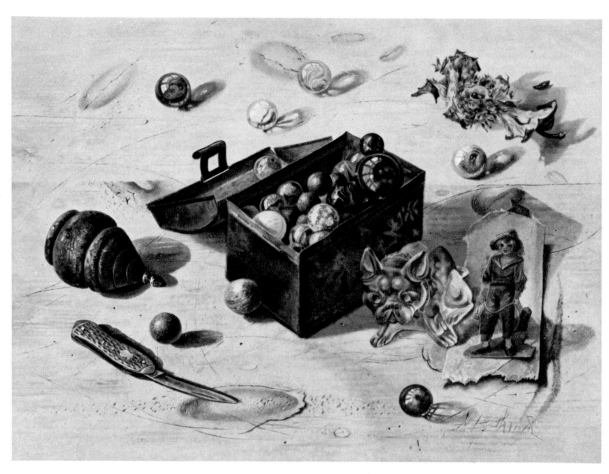

Treasure Chest, 1963, 9 x 12

Exercise with Seed Pods, 1963, 8 x 10

Bremen Town Musicians, 1964, 9 x 12

Water Nymphs, 1964, 9 x 12

Broken Doll, 1963, 10 x 8

facing, Queen of Kings, 1963, 20 x 16

French Doll, 1963, 8¾ x 7

Yellow Bird, 1963, 8¾ x 7

266

Blue Elephants, 1963, 16½ x 22½

Cast of Characters, 1963, 12½ x 22½

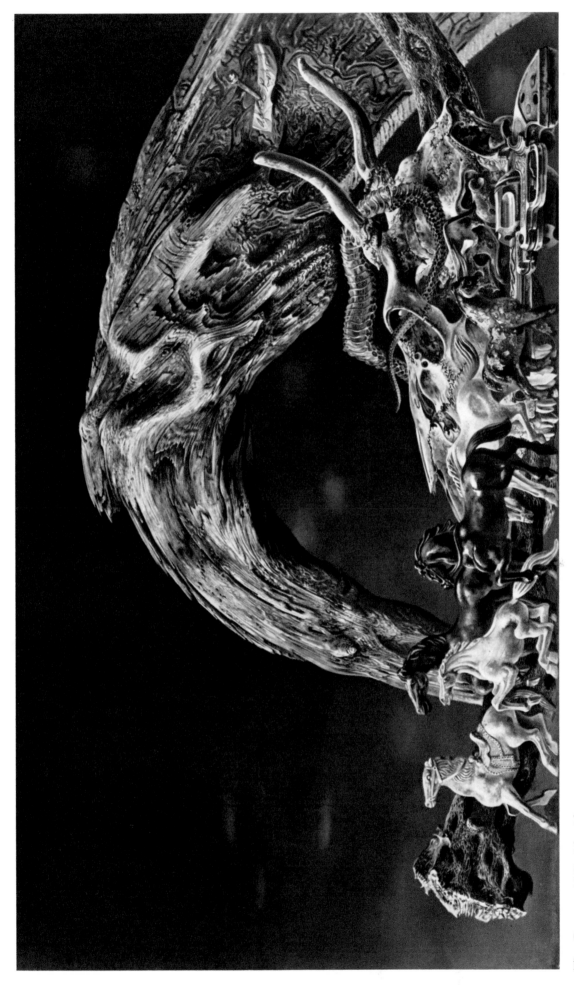

The Canyon, 1963, 14 x 24

269

The Decoy, 1963, 12 x 20

facing, The Frogs, 1964, 16 x 20

270

Little Egypt, 1964, 16 x 20

The Pit, 1964, 12 x 16

273

Sprouts, 1964, 16 x 12

Elephanta, 1964, 14⅝ x 10⅝

Hunters and Hunted, 1963, 12 x 9½

East and West, 1964, 12 x 9½

276

The Sporting Life, 1964, 14 x 20

Satyr, 1964, 9 x 6

Blue Boy, Green Girl, 1964, 9 x 6

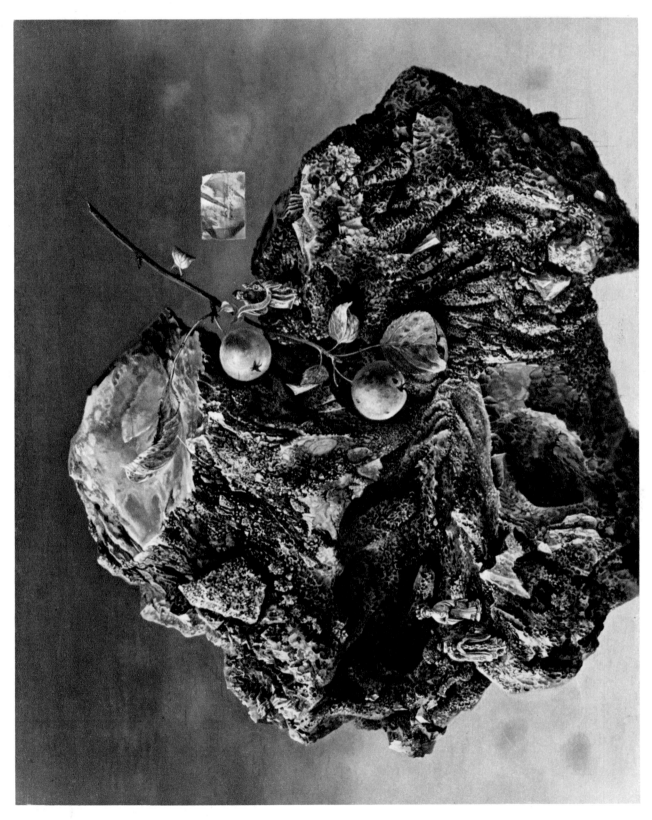

facing, Pastoral Still Life, 1964, 18 x 24

The Grotto, 1964, 16 x 20

281

Two Women, 1964, 16 x 12

Vermeer's Cook, 1964, 16 x 12

About Women, 1964, 16 x 12

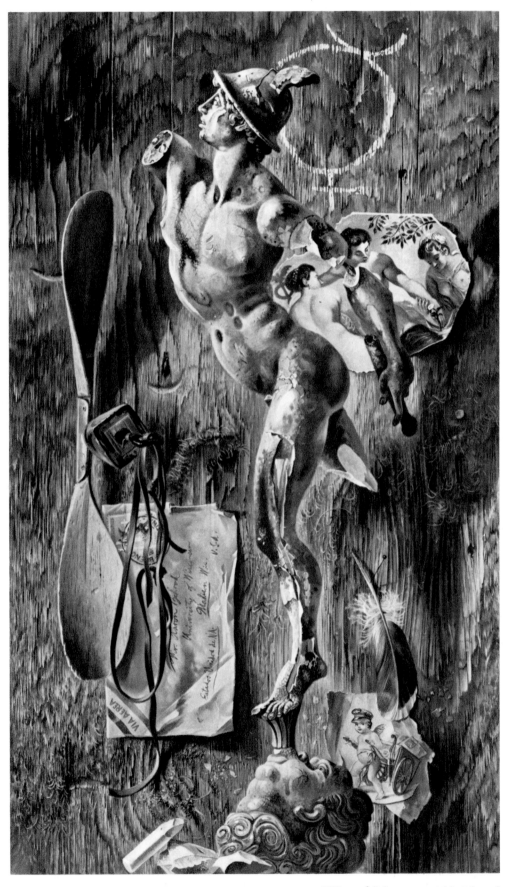

Winged Mercury, 1964, 24 x 14

Oriental Shelf, 1964, 12 x 24

facing, The Rowes, 1963–64, 24 x 32

"A" Is for Apple, 1964, 9 x 19

facing, Still Life with Goat, 1964, 10¾ x 14¾

Sign of the Mushroom, 1964, 16 x 12

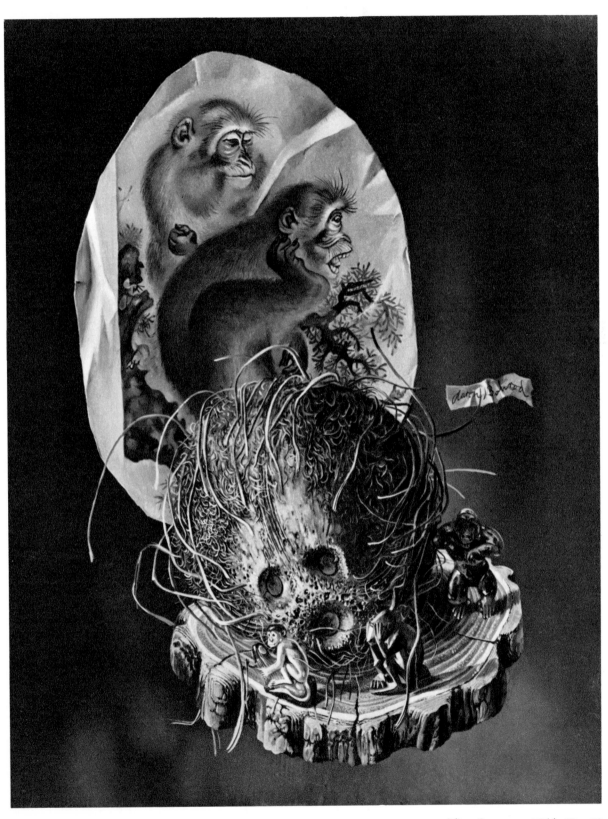

The Coconut, 1964, 13 × 10

Yorick, 1964, 12 x 16

Cowboy and Indian Corn, 1964, 12 x 16

Yesterday, Today, and Tomorrow, 1964, 9 x 12

Cakes, 1964, 10 x 13

295

With Love, 1964, 20 x 12

facing, A Ship of Fools, 1964, 21¾ x 15½

Fiesta de Toros, 1964–65, 16 x 20